Your Extraordinary Self

TAMMIE A KIP

Your Extraordinary Self
Copyright © 2019 by Tammie A Kip

All rights reserved. No part of this publication may be reproduced, distributed, or transmitted in any form or by any means, including photocopying, recording, or other electronic or mechanical methods, without the prior written permission of the author, except in the case of brief quotations embodied in critical reviews and certain other non-commercial uses permitted by copyright law.

Tellwell Talent
www.tellwell.ca

ISBN
978-0-2288-0472-7 (Paperback)
978-0-2288-0473-4 (eBook)

What Readers Are Saying About Your Extraordinary Self

"YOUR EXTRAORDINARY SELF was judged by top industry professionals—not as merely a great *indie* book—but as great book, period. Author Tammie A. Kip knows what's standing between you and your dreams—you!

Kip shows readers how to overcome obstacles, via sound advice and practical exercises for self-improvement in her book, which is packed with anecdotal evidence from a variety of great minds. Much of the advice in YOUR EXTRAORDINARY SELF has been offered before, but Kip has a winning way with words.

YOUR EXTRAORDINARY SELF encourages readers to plant the seeds of desire and watch what grows. Kip encourage readers to embrace the changes that stem from personal growth. Self-improvement is a long — often difficult — journey, but YOUR EXTRAORDINARY SELF makes it easier with practical advice and real-world exercises that change behaviors for the better. Kip's advice isn't new, but it's well told."

— Rob Errera for IndieReader

"This book is the thinking partner you always wished you could have. It is a guide to thinking strategies that are neither optimistic nor pessimistic, but rather possibilistic.

When you read this book, you can almost feel author Tammie Kip's warm hand on your back as she encourages you to fall in love with the possibilities that naturally exist within you and explore how to reach to make them realities."

*— Dawna Markova, Ph.D.,
author Reconcilable Differences,
CEO emeritus Professional Thinking Partners*

"This is an engaging book written without pretense, like a friend writing to a friend. There are helpful, pragmatic suggestions contained therein, not platitudes, but lessons to be learned and cherished. When you read it, you will find it was well worth your while; there is a lot of wisdom and potentially life changing advice dispensed with kindness."

*Richard Baseman
Chair, CEO Mentor/Advisor at Vistage Worldwide Inc*

Dedication

This book is dedicated to my two beautiful children, Jessica and Jacob. We have laughed together, cried together, grown together, and loved together. I am so proud of who you are and all you have yet to become. I wish nothing but happiness, success, and extraordinary lives for each of you today and every day until the end of time.

Thank you for your unwavering support, for always listening to my crazy ideas, and for believing in me. I love you both so much.

Table of Contents

Preface vii

1. Self, Meet Brain. Brain, Meet Self 1
2. The Power of Choice, It's Always Yours 23
3. Passion Fruit 41
4. Flip the Negative Switch to Off 59
5. Who am I today? 77
6. Gratitude's the New Attitude 97
7. Be Devilishly Selfish While Loving Others 121

About the Author 143
Bibliography 145
Notes 147

Preface

This book is not about looking at life through rose-coloured glasses or about helping you become the next Oprah Winfrey, Mark Zuckerberg, or Elon Musk. Although I admire all of them and many more successful people for all they have accomplished, we do not have to have that level of power or perception of success to be our best selves. Success is interpretive. How you define success may be different from how I define success and different from how your neighbour defines it or the kid down the road. I am not a world-famous philanthropist, psychologist, or entrepreneur, yet I feel I am living an extraordinary life because, for me, that means giving back where and how I can through charitable initiatives, working in my sweet spot, and giving a hundred percent every day. This means going to bed each night knowing I have added value to others in some way, shape, or form and waking up refreshed, excited for what's to come, singing in the morning, smiling frequently throughout the day, loving and being loved, and helping others feel the same. When my days, weeks, and months are filled with these things, then I know I am showing up in life as my best self which helps me feel contentment even when life throws those curveballs. Identifying what success means to you personally is the first step in getting to an extraordinary life, and I am hoping we can do that together.

This book was written for the sole purpose of inspiring, empowering, and encouraging people to recognize that they have the potential within to achieve their dreams, ambitions, and goals—even when life is not necessarily going their way.

We all have awesomeness in us; we just need to harness it, nurture it, develop it, and give ourselves permission to grow with it.

Because I have some awesome friends and people around me—people who truly live life to the fullest—I decided to tap into their knowledge to get their perspectives on what they do to live a fulfilled life and what tricks they use when life is not quite going their way or when they are having a bad day or week.

These are a broad range of people from my best friend, to entrepreneurs, lawyers, authors, executives, charity founders, renowned coaches, world travelers, and all-round good people (including my dad). I have met them through travels, business, social gatherings, and while in search of answers in my own life. I thought there would be a great deal of benefit to sharing their stories because; let's face it, what works for me may not work for you, and what works for you may not work for your sister or friend. The more tools we have and tips we can gather from others, the more we can test drive different strategies and mix and match to build our toolkits of awesomeness. It's like when retailers started to offer two-piece bathing suits and you could mix and match, or the M&M store in Time Square where you can grab a bag and fill it with all sorts of different M&Ms. Such a great concept—one size does not fit all! It is no different here.

Their stories will be infused throughout the chapters ahead. Feel free to copy, model, beg, steal, or borrow any and all of these tips and customize them to build the best version of you that you can be.

I cannot tell you what that looks like because only you know, but I can tell you that, when you are living out that version, you will be living an extraordinary life almost all of the time. Listen, if I can live out most of my days enjoying life to the fullest, being present every moment, feeling at peace whether I'm at a high point or low, then so can you. Seriously, if I can do it, *anyone* can do it! I guarantee you that this lens on life is much more beautiful and makes life a whole lot more fun.

We only get one life to live, so whether it is a great day or a horrible one, own it, live it, love it, and always remember #anythingspossible.

I have filled the book with some challenges to help you work through the concepts and apply them to your life as we discuss them. You may choose to do some or all of these challenges. I encourage you to have a separate notebook with you as you read the book. Write down the challenge number along with the page number in your notebook as you work through them. You may also want to go back to these challenges after finishing the book and putting some of these strategies into practice so you can see the change that has evolved within you.

This is going to be so much fun, so grab a notebook and a pen and let's get started with building that extraordinary life of yours!

1

Self, Meet Brain. Brain, Meet Self

Yesterday I was clever, so I wanted to change the world. Today I am wise, so I am changing myself.

—Rumi

That little thing called mindset

Life is hard. There are no two ways about it. We all have our difficulties. Sometimes we are at the top of our game and feel like we can conquer the world, and other times we may feel like we're drowning, and it takes everything in us to keep afloat. Although this book is about helping you become your best you—and for the most part is light and hopefully makes you laugh a little here and there—I want to share a relatively dark poem that I wrote when I was about fifteen.

> *Falling Apart*
>
> *The days grow warmer as the year goes on*
> *The nights grow darker and seem too long*
> *The water seems colder*
> *The air seems to smolder*
> *My world is falling apart*
>
> *Not enough time to do everything*
> *The pain of the world just seems to sting*
> *There's no one there to give me support*
> *No one there with whom to retort*
> *My freedom is falling apart*
>
> *Lying awake on a bed of steel*
> *No one to look to, no one to feel*
> *I close my eyes and pray for a tomorrow*
> *Minus the heartache and minus the sorrow*
> *My life is falling apart ....*

Now you may be wondering, why on earth is she sharing this, and what can I possibly learn from someone whose world is falling apart? I share this with you because this was my fifteen-year-old self, writing through her teenage lens. What teenager do you know whose life was not falling apart at one point or another? It was a period of my life where I clearly felt things were not going very well for me—I stress the words *I felt* because, on the outside, anyone would have said I was a happy, well-adjusted, intelligent teen who had everything going for her. On the inside, clearly, this was not the case in my reality.

Human beings are volatile creatures. One day we can be up, and the next day we may be down. The trick is to have more highs than lows, pick ourselves up quickly when we fall, forgive ourselves and others, believe that we are enough, and continually move forward in our lives, not back. This has everything to do with our mindset and how we are wired.

Our mindset is a state of being and houses our beliefs. Beliefs drive our behaviours, and our behaviours affect our decisions. To change our behaviours, we must first change our beliefs.

My fifteen-year-old self believed her world was falling apart. This was due to the mindset I was in at the time which was telling me I wasn't good enough, I wasn't smart enough, I wasn't skinny enough, I wasn't pretty enough. I wasn't enough. To change my doom-and-gloom outlook on life (my behaviour), I had to change my beliefs about being enough. Now although, way back then, I did not understand the semantics of this, I did recognize that this was not how I wanted my permanent outlook on life to be, and so it began.

The Things We Tell Ourselves

Self-limiting beliefs and self-doubt are the biggest obstacles we face in achieving our goals and dreams. This can even occur despite proven records of accomplishment and past successes. Whether or not we have done work on quashing those beliefs, they can and do come back from time to time. When they do, we must recognize them for what they are—pure nonsense. We must take time to reflect on why they are showing up in our lives at the time they are, acknowledge the feelings they are provoking and allow ourselves to release them, as they are not serving us. Why hold on to something that is bringing you down? It's like going swimming in the ocean with a brick. How much more difficult is it to stay afloat with that brick in your hands? As soon as you release it, everything becomes lighter and you can float almost effortlessly. The longer it has been weighing you down, the lighter you feel when you finally let it go.

The same goes for these beliefs we hold on to that serve absolutely no purpose. Now, I know what you're thinking. *That's all fine and dandy, Tammie, but these beliefs have been hard-wired into me, how can I just let them go?* Don't worry, we will get there, I promise. First a little personal story that will hopefully resonate with some of you.

The year 2013 was very difficult for me. I was in year five of my business, and the industry I was working in had changed drastically. Revenue and profitability were in a downward spiral yet I was being nominated for two separate and very prestigious leadership awards, one of which I was awarded. I felt like a fraud and cringed every time someone congratulated me or spoke of how *successful* I was. In my mind, I was a failure.

I spent some time talking to one of my very close friends about all of this and how I felt. For my birthday that year, she bought me Sheryl Sandberg's book *Lean In* and wrote this beautiful note on the inside cover:

> *I was thinking of our talk the other day and remembered some words that I had read in this book. I have marked the pages for you. I just want you to know that so many times in my life and especially over the last few years in my current role as a "business expert", I find that I question, am I really an expert? Business associates come to me all day long asking for my opinions and suggestions and I think, really me, I'm the expert? Part of me feeling like a fraud, like someone will find out that I am not an expert, that the jig will be up! When I read this book, I had my own little ah ha moment and knew that I was not alone. I thought it may be helpful for you and that you would really love this book. Just so you know, you are an amazing, smart, talented, innovative woman. That is no fraud! You are as real and genuine as a person can possibly be, and there are so many reasons that people look up to you. You may make mistakes, but you learn from them. You may have tough times, but they make you stronger and wiser and that is why we look up to you my friend.*

Her kind words made me cry, not the pain kind of cry, the "feel-good" kind of cry. Even to this day, when I read them, I am still choked up. She was right. The book really did get me out of my "fraud" slump. Although I still felt unworthy of the praise I continued to receive while things continued to downward spiral, it just motivated me that much more to come out of it and do something even more amazing. Although I had wanted to write a book for a number of years, Sheryl's book really resonated with me. Not just because of the things she wrote but also because of why she wrote it. It was exactly why I wanted to write as well. Mine is a similar message with a different delivery. I am certainly no Sheryl Sandberg; I am simply a regular woman with somewhat normal children who lives a relatively ordinary life with whom most of the population can relate. Once I was able to quash the belief that I was a fraud, I regained my perspective on the life I wanted to continue to live.

You will hear me use the word *perspective* quite a bit during our time together, and that is because I cannot stress enough that everything we see, everything we say, and everything we do is translated, received or heard in a different way depending on the perspective we ourselves or others are viewing it from. I used to have this discussion with a former boyfriend of mine. I loved him dearly, but he was one of the most opinionated people I had ever met. If others did not see things his way, they were just plain wrong. I would never argue with him about anything—I would simply say one of two things: either "that's your opinion" or "this is my perspective." You can never argue with someone's perspective because, for all intents and purposes, that is their reality, and who are we to question someone's reality?

How we speak to ourselves and what we tell ourselves dictates who we become. I spent some time in San Diego a few years back at a training session with a group of coaches. We did not know each other going in, but by the end of the program, we had become quite close. Although there were many inspirational people within our cohort, I connected with two in particular, largely because I was so inspired by them. One of those individuals is John Fenton, author of 5 *Minute Mastery: The Surprising Secrets for Transforming Your Stress to Success and Mastering What is Important.* He is a renowned coach, speaker, and friend. You know when you meet someone and immediately you can tell they are truly authentic? You feel you can share anything with them because they themselves are not afraid to be vulnerable and are free from judgement. Well, John is that person. Although we had not talked much since our training together, when I reflected on who I was going to approach to share some tips on how to be your best self, John was top of mind. I am very grateful that he agreed to be interviewed, and in true John fashion, he came through with some wonderful words of wisdom. John shared a story with me about a part of his journey that prompted him to make some changes in his life at a young age.

In his adolescence, John was not very athletic. In the US in the late sixties and into the seventies, physical fitness was an important part of the junior high school education systems, and each year The President's Physical Fitness Award was recognized for those students who excelled athletically. The junior high school that he attended was proud to have awarded the most Presidents Fitness Awards of any school in their county. The students would go through a series of physical tests and be awarded based on their scores and then placed into groups according to how well they did. The gold award was the highest honour of the President's Physical Fitness Award, and winners received a gold card and patch for their sweater; the second group received a blue card, and the third group received a red card—and of course, the kids who did not rate in any of these categories received nothing. It was like the Marine Corps; the phys-ed class was platooned based on their fitness levels, and each group wore a coloured tee-shirt to signify their level of success. The gold award winners wore gold tee-shirts, the blue card recipients wore blue, and the red card recipients wore red. For everyone else, the ones who did not succeed at any level, they wore white tee-shirts.

The gold boys called the white shirts cream puffs. At the time, John was about thirty pounds overweight and wearing a white shirt. It was in that moment he vowed that he was no longer going to run in the back of the pack and that he was going to win that fitness award the next year. He decided at that moment that he mattered. He was not any less of a person because he was not wearing a gold shirt. It was then that he decided to shift his mindset from the victim mentality that had been holding him back.

From here, John went on to be a football scholar, a successful businessperson, a husband, and a father. Later on in life, John had another pivotal moment that led him to leave his successful career and take an early retirement to pursue his passion. I encourage you to read all about John's journey in his book, *5 Minute Mastery*.

John's story resonates with so many and falls in line quite beautifully with this section of the book on mindset and how we talk to ourselves. When we play the victim, we are the victim. When we tell ourselves that we matter, that we are the makers of our own destiny, only then can we truly begin to master our lives and be the best version of ourselves we can be. Another important take-away here is that our lives are full of pivots. What causes you to go in a certain direction at one point in your life may not necessarily work at another. Reflection and awareness (both of which we discuss later) are two key sources of power that will help guide you during those pivotal times in your life.

Take a moment to think about how you talk to yourself, and yes, I do actually verbally talk to myself. Some may say that's crazy, but I find when I verbalize my self-talk, it has much more of an impact than if I just think it. When I tell myself "I got this," I really nail it. When I think it, this tends to allow competing thoughts to enter my headspace. I can only physically say one thing at a time, but my mind can think a dozen things at once. I challenge you, next time negative self-talk enters your mind, verbalize the opposite. Say it, repeat, believe it, and live it. This will trump the voices in your head every time!

<u>Challenge #1</u>

Think of a self-limiting belief you have about your ability to do something then describe three to five reasons why you **can** do it, for example:

Self-limiting belief: I cannot stand up in front of a group to give a presentation; I get too nervous public speaking.

Affirmations to the contrary: I am knowledgeable when it comes to the content, I am thoroughly prepared, and I am with a group of my peers.

Train don't drain that brain

From the time we are newborns and all through life, we are taught **what** to think, not **how** to think. Take a moment to reflect on your upbringing. For the most part, our parents conditioned us to listen to our teachers, to go with the flow, be a part of the norm, and not to cause waves. We went to school, and attended class when the bell rang. We sat with twenty to thirty other kids in the classroom while the teacher stood at the front of the room teaching us about history, math, English, and science. Our knowledge was gauged by quizzes, tests, exams, and papers—all of which had right or wrong answers. We were taught what to think. Not how to think.

In fact, when ideas were expressed that did not fit within the tidy little box that was the curriculum, they were often dismissed as nonsense and the source of those ideas was promptly redirected back to the text or learning of the day. Now, I must admit, postsecondary curricula have come a long way, and most now offer a creative space for new ideas and innovative thinking, encouraging growth beyond scientific and statistical norms. That being said, in our early years, we are still subject to very traditional methods of being taught what to think, and these are the impressionable years when we start to develop our beliefs, which as we well know, drive our behaviours.

Imagine a world where we are taught how to think. What would that look like?

Education is a cornerstone of society. It should be interesting and engaging. It provides us with all sorts of knowledge, but the actual teaching of how to think is missing. When we are involved in the process of own learning, we engage our minds by questioning things. When we learn how to think about something, it sparks curiosity in our brain, and we become vested in the learning. This fuels the creativity in us. Now when I refer to creativity, I am not talking about artwork or musical creativity, I am referring to the creativity within our minds—creative thinking. This thinking allows us to innovate and solve problems. We should never trust our brains at first instance because we are prone to cognitive biases. We are all to some extent flawed, ignorant, and deluded. We may think that we do not hold a bias, but in reality, subconscious bias exists in all of us whether we choose to believe it or not. Critical thinking teaches us how to process things effectively and helps to mitigate any unconscious bias. When we are critical thinkers, we become much more aware. When a mind is trained to think creatively and critically, the mind expands, grows, explores, and helps us achieve what was once thought to be the impossible.

Sir Ken Robinson has a wonderful TED Talk entitled "Do Schools Kill Creativity?"[1] In it, he explains that all kids have tremendous talent, and we squander it. Creativity is as important as literacy and should be treated with the same status. Kids are not afraid of being wrong. If you are not prepared to be wrong, you will never come up with anything original. Our education system is not conducive to children being wrong. He says we do not grow into creativity; we are educated out of it. We all start out being creative.

Robinson shares with us that there are three things about intelligence:

1. *Intelligence is diverse. We think about the world in the way we experience it; visually, in sound and kinetically. We think in the abstract, and we think in movement.*
2. *Intelligence is dynamic. It is wonderfully interactive. Our brain is divided into departments. Creativity is an original idea that has value and comes from the different ways we see things.*
3. *Intelligence is distinct. Everyone thinks idiosyncratically and has their own exceptional intelligence that feeds into their unique talent and abilities.*

We need to rethink the fundamental principles in which we are being educated. We need to appreciate the gift of human imagination and use it wisely. We must see our creative capacity for the richness that it is, must see our children for the promise they represent and help them make something of it by encouraging them how to think, not what to think. And while we are at it, we need to do the same for ourselves.

A fun fact—typically the morning is the best time to be creative. It is the time of day when the prefrontal cortex is most active. A scientific study of brain circuits confirmed that this creative activity is highest during and immediately after sleep, while the analytical parts of the brain (the editing and proofreading parts) become more active as the day goes on.

Our mindset dictates how we see things. If we operate with a closed mindset, we are more likely to believe that something cannot be done. Conversely, if we are leaning towards the open end of the mindset scale, we are more apt to believe that things can be done. Basically, whether you think you can or you think you can't, you're right! The way we think of ourselves and our ability to do something directly affects our results.

James Allen's book *As a Man Thinketh* launched the self-help movement way back in 1903. His book speaks to how thoughts control behaviour and the effect that thoughts have on our circumstances and life.

> *As the physically weak man can make himself strong by careful and patient training, so the man of weak thoughts can make them strong by exercising himself in right thinking.*
>
> —James Allen

What a powerful statement.

Let us think about that for a moment. What Allen is saying is that we can train our minds just like we can train our bodies. Taking this one-step further, let us start with the mind and the body will follow. All of our spiritual or emotional thoughts manifest themselves into physical form. If we go through life telling ourselves that we cannot do something, the physical output correlates with that of our thoughts. If we focus our efforts and energy into making something happen, the physical manifestation will have no choice but to reflect that which we desire. Now, just to be clear, this is not as simple as wishing something to happen then it becomes true. It is about planting the seed of desire. Setting a specific goal of what you want to achieve by when and then developing a plan to achieve that goal. When we write out the plan and desired results and recite the plan and desires daily, we are planting seeds in our subconscious mind. At this point, the mind has no option but to start to present ideas to you as to how to achieve your goals. Some call this intuition or coincidences and others call it fate. I know this may seem a little heavy to some, but if you can grasp and accept this concept, that is half the battle.

For example, let's say you want to get into the best physical shape of your life this year. You do all the things to start off right. You research meal plans, an exercise regime, join a gym and maybe even hire a personal trainer and a nutritionist. You start gung-ho because you have put all the physical elements in place, but it does not last. Why is that? Well, beliefs drive behaviour. Did you train your mind to believe that this is how you want to live, or did you simply make the decision to get into shape without planting the seeds of change? Without training your mind, it will operate based on what it knows, and what it knows, in this case, is what has always been.

Though our brain is not a muscle, it is scientifically proven that we can continue to develop and train our brains through *mental exercise*. Our brain may not grow bigger like our biceps when we hit the gym, but we can develop new neural connections and make them stronger than ever. In essence, we can re-wire our brains, or if you prefer, we can teach an old dog new tricks!

A study conducted by Duke University suggests that 45 percent of our behaviour stems from habit. Bestselling author Charles Duhigg tells us that the process within our brains that creates habits is a three-step loop. First, there is a **cue**, a trigger that tells your brain to go into automatic mode and which habit to use. Then there is the **routine**, which can be physical, mental, or emotional. Finally, there is a **reward**, which helps your brain figure out if this particular loop is worth remembering for the future. Over time, this loop—cue, routine, reward, cue, routine, reward—becomes more and more automatic.

The cue and reward become neurologically intertwined until a sense of craving emerges. Habits are deeply rooted into our subconscious mind. In order to change the habit, we must change our belief about the trigger and resulting reward. For example, if we believe that having a drink will eliminate or reduce stress, then we need to think of alternative ways to address the stress.

Self-talk, reflection, positive affirmations, and daily practice are keys to changing your beliefs and therefore your behaviour.

I used to work with this lovely woman many moons ago. I was a branch manager, involved in the operations of the company, and she worked in our Montreal office in the IT department. Management information and big data were just starting to enter our industry, so we were working on ways to improve our systems to not only capture the data our clients required but to deliver it in a format that was useful for them. We spent many hours in meetings together with other managers in the organization and 90 percent of the time, when we asked whether the system could be enhanced to capture certain data, the response, in her French accent, was "it cannot be done." If I had a dime for every time I heard "it cannot not be done," I would be a very wealthy woman.

Why could it not be done? Other companies and people were doing it, our customers required it, and although we were not technically a technology company, an IT firm owned us. There was no reason it could not be done other than the fact that this is what was hard-wired into this lovely woman's brain.

Renowned leadership expert, John Maxwell shared a story at one of his international certification training events I attend regularly, and it spoke so beautifully to this concept. He spoke of a time he was in Australia with his wife Margaret and another couple. They were on a privately chartered cruise, and the guide was telling them that the Australian open was taking place that day. John mentioned that he would love to go see it. The charter explained that it was impossible to get tickets. Well if you know John Maxwell, you know what his reaction to *that* would be. Nothing is impossible if you want it bad enough.

As they continued on their cruise, they came upon the location of the Open. When the charter mentioned that they were approaching the area where the open was taking place that day, John asked the rest of the group if they were interested in trying to get in to see the match. None of them were. He asked if they minded if he tried, and no, they didn't mind, so John asked the charter to let him off. She told him she would wait because he would not be able to get a ticket and did not want to leave him stranded, but he told them to go on, he would be fine.

He went to the ticket counter to see if he could purchase a ticket. He was told that tickets had been sold out for a very long time so there was none available. He saw people lined up inside the gate and asked what that was all about. He was told that it was a standby line for when ticketholders are not able to make the event but that the chances of getting a ticket there were slim although he was welcome to try. He was thrilled to move beyond the gate and into the facilities.

He took his place in line, which was just over a hundred people from the front. He knew he was going to have to get a lot closer than that, so he started talking to some people in the front of the line expressing how anxious he was to see the match and how he would gladly pay for their ticket if they would bring him in with them. This did not pan out, so he decided to move closer to the event to see what other options there were.

As he did this, a woman was walking away from the event. She happened upon John and explained that she had to leave and could not attend the match. She asked if he wanted her ticket. Well of course, he accepted this gracious offer, paid her for the ticket and walked to his seat— which was within the first few rows—and watched the event that was impossible to get into.

Now some people will hear this story and think *wow, was he ever lucky*. But was he? Sure, perhaps there is an *element* of luck here, but if he'd taken what the charter said about the event being impossible to get into at face value, he never would have tried. If he had stopped at the first window when he was told the tickets were sold out, he would never have gotten past the first gate. If he'd gave up when he was 102 in the standby line, he would not have meandered towards the event. He was determined. He wanted to see the match, so he was determined to find a way to do it, and he did.

What does all of this mean for us? How do we use our mind to become healthier, happier, and better tomorrow than we are today? Well, you are well on your way! By choosing to take time to invest in yourself and reading books just like this, you are making the choice to live an extraordinary life.

So before we conclude this chapter, let us look at some final things we can do to tap into that big, beautiful brain of yours.

Challenge #2

Take time to get to you know you. This may sound simple or even somewhat silly, but the more in tune you are with yourself, the easier and quicker you will be able to identify when you are at your best. If you are a morning person, then this is when your brain is at its best. If a night owl then you will be more apt to have higher outputs later in the day. Reserve this high output time to tackle the tasks that require brainpower. Do not waste this precious time on scanning social media, watching TV, or reading the paper. There is a time and place for these things if you so choose; however, that time is not when your brain is at its optimal peak performance level.

Reflect on the past few days and describe the time of day that you felt the most productive and why. If you cannot isolate the times, pay close attention to the upcoming days and come back to do this exercise.

Challenge #3

Stop looking at incidents in isolation. If you procrastinate on that home or school project you have been meaning to start, you may think to yourself, it's just one day, I will make it up tomorrow. This type of thinking leads us to treat events as though they are disconnected from everything else, which is contrary to reality. These decisions do not affect one incident or one moment in time, they affect the person you become. Author T. Harv Eker highlights the significance of this habit in his book, *Secrets of the Millionaire Mind*:

> "How you do anything is how you do everything."

I love that quote. When you look at incidents in isolation, you tend to be more lenient on yourself, which leads to a repeat in behaviour and eventually forms a habit. So the next time you tell yourself, it is just this one time, think about how the action—or lack thereof—will affect your big-picture life and goals.

Describe a time you exhibited this type of behaviour and what came of it. For example, deciding not to prepare your lunch one night before work, causing you to buy your lunch the next day, then again the day after, and the day after that. Before you know it, you bought your lunch the whole week, causing you to spend unnecessary money and eat less healthy.

—

We will discuss awareness a little later on in the book, which will help us work through what to do when we identify these behaviours. The first step is understanding the fundamentals and acknowledging them when they occur. Congratulations on completing this first step!

The Power of Choice, It's Always Yours

You have brains in your head, you have feet in your shoes, you can steer yourself in any direction you choose.

—Dr. Seuss

Crossroads

I used to be a smoker. I started smoking when I was way too young and smoked for almost twenty years.

I tried to stop smoking a number of times. So many times, in fact, that I became somewhat of an expert on quitting, but I always seemed to go back to it. I always had an excuse. Stress, work issues, weight gain, whatever the excuse, the smoking was a crutch for me. At one point I thought I could be a social smoker. I would smoke when out with friends and while having a drink or two, but that just went from bad to worse. I was on the verge of becoming a raging alcoholic in addition to a smoker! I found myself making a drink just so I could have a cigarette. Clearly *social smoking* was not the answer me.

I knew there were plenty of reasons to quit: I did not want my children growing up in a household with a mother who smoked. The cost of cigarettes was rising. I knew smoking was bad for me. Above all, I was angry. I am a bit of a control freak, and the fact that I had no control over whether or not I smoked—the fact that *it* controlled *me*—is what bothered me most.

I heard that hypnosis had helped some people quit smoking. This intrigued me. After all, I had already tried everything else, what did I have to lose? Now the thing with hypnosis is that you have to be hypnotizable. Fortunately—or unfortunately, depending on how you look at it—I knew for a fact that I could be hypnotized because, in my younger years, I was one of those crazy people who volunteered to get up on stage during a Yuk Yuks comedy night featuring a hypnotist (but that's a story for another day). Suffice it to say, my susceptibility to hypnosis was not in question, so I decided to take the plunge.

I remember the day clearly. It was a Monday morning. I do not remember all of the words that were said, but I do recall the part that I think of as the crossroads. It is as vivid in my mind today, as it was that day so many years ago. I was deep under, my arms heavy, and all of my actions felt as if they were in slow motion. I was walking in a forest, alone with no purpose or intended destination, just following the path when I came along a break in the trail. To the right of me was a path that was dark, dingy, lined with garbage and cigarette butts, still water, and a grey bleak sky. To the left was a beautiful path filled with colourful flowers, tall trees with lustrous green leaves, lively wildlife, running creeks and a rainbow. At this exact moment, the hypnotist asked me to choose my path.

As I stood at the crossroads and pondered each of the paths, I knew the choice I was about to make was about more than just quitting smoking. I knew whichever path I chose would be my path for life. Did I want to live a dingy life that controlled me or a glorious life which I controlled?

As I took my first step towards the beautiful bright rainbow path, tears of joy streamed down my cheeks. I left the hypnotist's office that day, and not only did I never crave another cigarette again, I noticed a remarkable difference in how I chose to live my life. No more "what ifs", "I wonder what would have happened had I" or "I wish I would have", all because of the power of choice. Now don't get me wrong, I have made many mistakes in my life, some of them so good I've even made them twice, but I choose not to have regrets because every time I've made a choice, it's exactly what I wanted at that specific moment in time.

Most people let life happen to them as though they were a passenger in their own car. Imagine what your life would look like if you assumed the driver's seat and took the wheel in your own two hands, if you chose to be intentional each day instead of submissive, if you used words such as "I will" instead of "I hope to", "action" over "desire", "today" instead of "someday", if you chose to be active rather than passive.

We all come to crossroads in our lives and struggle with which path to choose. The important thing to know is that you have a choice, and whether it is the right path or the learning one, you must be intentional about your choice and choose the path that allows you to be the driver of your own car. Remember, we tend not to regret the decisions we make—we regret those decisions that we fail to make or allow others to make on our behalf.

You will not always have the opportunity to gain clarity through a hypnosis session to guide you to the answer (if you even believe in that practice at all), so it is important to have a decision-making process to guide you. The decision-making process is unique to everyone, so it is something only you can create, but here are some things to get you thinking about what might work for you:

1. Define the problem, challenge, or opportunity
2. Think of the possible implications in each scenario
3. Discuss and brainstorm with your inner circle, mentors, and/or advisors
4. Identify and negate self-limiting thoughts that may impact your decision
5. Evaluate the pros and cons associated with each option
6. Make the choice which aligns most with your passion, values, and goals *without* regard to fears, inhibitions, or naysayers
7. Implement the option chosen

8. Be persistent
9. Reflect on the decision and modify course of action as needed

Who's the matter with me today?

How many times have you heard a person blame a situation on someone else or circumstance? Have many times have you done this yourself? Do you find yourself continually looking for someone or something else to blame when things go wrong?

We all encounter circumstances (or people) that may throw a wrench into best-laid plans, but ultimately, they are not responsible for your outcomes. Only you hold that card.

Two main things happen when we deflect blame. One, we do not realize that we are part of the problem, and two, we tend not to be solution focused. After all, it's not our problem!

A similar analogy would be like when your company holds a "refresher" session on a protocol because a few people are not following it. Ironically, the reason for the refresher is for the few, but it is those exact few who think they do not have to attend because it doesn't apply to them. This is no different. When we stop looking to others to blame and start looking within, we begin taking greater control and ownership over the outcome of our lives and create positive change within ourselves and for others.

When you become more aware and accept the fact that you are the only one responsible for your actions and outcomes and, further, that you and you alone have the power to choose, things will start to change for you. In the last chapter we talked about mindset. Mindset is a choice. There are very few things we have explicit control over in our lives; the ability to make a choice is one of those things.

Once we accept this power, the power of choice, we can choose to expand our minds and change anything for the better, including our habits.

> Challenge #4
>
> Think of a time you had a choice to make. What was the process you used to work through the decision? Describe how this process would differ now and how it may have affected the outcome of your decision.

—

> Challenge #5
>
> Consider a situation where you blamed someone or some circumstance for the outcome. Now reflect on that situation and determine what you could have done to positively affect the outcome regardless of the circumstances you were working with.

—

A change will do you good.

When was the last time you did something for the first time? How did it make you feel—nervous, fearful, insecure, invigorated, or grateful? Perhaps a little of all of the above.

Many people fear change and, therefore, fight it. And why *wouldn't* they—after all, our internal predispositions teach us to resist change, mainly so we can maintain a certain element of control over our environment.

I would say I have always tried to embrace change for the opportunity it brings, but even with that mindset, there have been times in my years that I opted for complacency over growth due to fear of the unknown. I have been taught and believe that our mindset controls our behaviours, and our behaviours control our outcomes. If you choose to live with a growth mindset, you will evolve as a person, as a loved one, and as a leader. This does not mean that every decision you make will be the right one, nor does it guarantee success. In fact, change may ultimately lead to failure, but if you have not failed, you have not grown.

Change leads to a world of possibility. It stretches the mind and feeds the soul. It leads us to opportunities that we didn't know existed and stimulates the curiosity part of our brain. There are numerous benefits associated with enhancing our curiosity. It has been medically proven that curiosity serves as a form of motivation. The more curious we are, the more we want to learn.

In a study published in the journal *Neuron*, researchers found that people who were curious about a subject learned more and remembered more than those that were not as curious. Not only did they learn more and remember more about the subject, they also remembered more about unrelated things such as faces in the room and learned information quicker than the others. The part I like best is that researchers found when people were more curious about the subject, their dopamine activity increased, which among other things, is the part of the brain that makes you happy. Then, once you get into the ramped-up state of dopamine, it interacts with the brain's hippocampus—the part of your brain that makes new memories—and the magic begins. This interaction increases your ability to learn, create new memories, retain information, and basically puts your brain into a sponge state so it soaks up everything. Good times!

It used to drive me crazy when my children were young and would ask the proverbial "why" question relentlessly. They demanded an answer for everything. They wanted to know the motivation behind every action, the reason behind every decision, and the rationales for all of life's mysteries. Well my children are well beyond those "why" years now, and unfortunately, for them, I was not as aware as I am today, so many of those "why" questions went unanswered. Now however, when my niece and nephew or any little person for that matter ask me the "whys" of the world, I am much more willing to encourage their curiosity. After all, who am I to stifle all that beautiful dopamine and activated hippocampi! But I digress, back to embracing change.

If we want to move forward in our lives, we must evolve, and how we evolve is a choice. We are the drivers of our personality, cognitive capabilities, emotions, and actions. Life is always about more than what happens *to* you, it is also about your perception and reaction to the circumstances you are dealing with. The evolution of our being is intrinsically associated with how we choose to accept and adapt to change.

Change offers us an opportunity to grow, to learn from our mistakes, to celebrate our successes, and to continually feed into our insatiable desire to improve upon ourselves and live an extraordinary life. However, we must remember that not all change equals growth. If you move to the left, your position has changed, but you have not moved forward. It is not until you intentionally put one foot in *front* of the other that change will guide you towards growth.

Fulfilment comes in all shapes and sizes. What gives one person a sense of fulfilment will not be the same for everyone else. One thing is common for certain—although you will experience fulfilment during the course of your life, it will not last without a willingness to change, evolve, and grow. As my friend, John Maxwell says, change will lead you to growth if you do it willingly or to grief if you do it reluctantly.

So the next time you are faced with change, I encourage you to embrace it as the gift it is and take the opportunity to evolve and grow. Your future self will thank you!

Challenge #6

Think of a time where you were forced to change something in your life that you did not want to change. Reflect on how you handled that change then describe how you *could* have handled it differently by embracing it as an opportunity.

Stuck in the middle

We all get stuck every now and again. Making the choice to work through our inertia as opposed to giving up will ultimately help in leading us to success. If we give up every time we hit a roadblock, we will have very little sense of accomplishment in our lives.

Being stuck can take on many different forms of varying levels. It could be a feeling of not being inspired, of not knowing what to do next, of sitting in front of a blank computer screen trying to finish that paper for class, loss of focus of our goals, or questioning our values. Being stuck can be so intense at times that it begins to take form as our new *normal*. Before we can get unstuck, we have to understand where we are. What is our present point of arrival? If we do not know where we are, we do not have a departure point from which to leave. Whether you are a little stuck or in a life funk—which is how I refer to long-term stuckedness—the first step in determining your present arrival point is reflection.

When we reflect, it gives us an opportunity to think about our intentions. If you are stuck with one of your goals or on a project, think about when you set the goal or the object of the project. What is the purpose? Think deeper into the reason and ask yourself questions that will help you to clarify your intent. The better the questions you ask of yourself, the better the answers will be. If you're stuck in a life funk, reflection will help you. It allows you to go back to a point in time where you can experience the emotions associated with the life you want to live. It helps clarify your dreams, your values, and what it feels like to be your best you. It helps you get beyond the past and allows you to focus on the now and the future. During reflection, allow yourself to be quiet and calm. Find a space without interruptions and focus solely on reflecting. Often when you allow yourself the opportunity to have uninterrupted time with yourself to think things through, answers and solutions will present themselves.

Dr. Lani Nelson Zlupko has a wonderful TED Talk called "Staying Stuck or Moving Forward"[2]. In it, she talks about how we look at our problems because, often times when we are stuck, it is as a result of problems we are facing. When we look at problems through a problem-focused lens, we ask ourselves problem-focused questions. Moreover, when we ask ourselves problem-focused questions, we get problem-focused answers, for example, "What is wrong with me, why can I not get this project started?" The answers we inevitability tell ourselves will be negative around our ability to complete the project, for example, "because I'm not good enough" –or– "I don't know enough" –or– "It's over my head." This type of thinking serves no purpose and will not help us get past our problem. We need to ask ourselves solution-focused questions, for example, "What will help me get started?" Perhaps then, answers will look more like "Just type whatever comes to mind" –or– "Think of a similar situation and how you handled it then use those tools" –or– "talk it out with a mentor or friend." It is amazing what happens when we change the questions we ask of ourselves.

Dr. Zlupko also shares that talking about a problem for too long is harmful rather than helpful. Yes, we need to talk about the problem at the beginning to sort through it, understand it, and share it—but then we must move on. We need to work on diminishing the problem, and we cannot do that if we dwell on it.

There was a time in my life during which I was severely stuck. This was more than just "I haven't written a blog in months" stuck –or– "I'm not achieving my goals this quarter" stuck. This stuck hijacked my life and consumed me to the point of physical manifestation which lead to a nervous breakdown.

Let me tell you about it.

During his early teenage years, my son had severe anxiety, did poorly in school as a result, and turned to self-medication to help him get through the pain of life as he knew it. Needless to say, this was a very difficult couple of years for the whole family. Battles with school boards, countless hours of research on how and where to get him the help he needed, and several court appearances for the related criminal charges that he invariably encountered because of his drug-induced behaviour. Every day was filled with worry that the police would come to the door to tell me he was in jail, in the hospital, or worse.

In addition to this, several other things in life were pretty dismal too. I was in one of those periods governed by Murphy's Law, where everything that *could* go wrong *seemed* to go wrong. I did everything any mother would do. Counselling, school meetings, house rules, groundings, you name it. Nothing seemed to work. I was stuck. Obviously, I had been stuck before, but this was different. This was one of the biggest challenges I had ever faced. This was my son, my baby, my beautiful little munchkin who meant the world to me. His life was falling apart right in front of my eyes, and it seemed there was nothing I could do to help him.

I did not realize the toll this was taking on me until one day it became very evident. I had just spent almost $4,000 to fix my car. The day after I picked it up, I was driving home, and the drive train let go. I was relatively close to home, so I managed to get the car there, but the whole way home after it happened, I could not stop crying. It was the straw that broke the camel's back, so to speak. By the time I got home, I was in full-out hysteria. I could not even walk. I literally *crawled* into the house and into my bed. My son was home and saw me in this state. He did not know what to do. Through my hysteria, I managed to utter the words…

"Call Uncle David."

My sister-in-law and brother rushed to my side. I could not breathe. I was having convulsions and was close to completely blacking out. This went on for what seemed to be an eternity. They had no choice but to call the ambulance. I was broken.

A woman who had conquered many mountains, built businesses, continually gave back to the community, and who could once handle anything that life threw her way with dignity, grace, and a smile was curled up in a fetal position on her bed in a spasmodic state. I could not even speak and was at a loss as to what to do next. I spent that whole weekend alone in my house in bed simply due to an extreme lack of energy; I could not move, eat, or communicate with anyone. As horrible as it felt at the time, it was an opportunity for me to take the time I needed to reflect and work through my current state of stuckedness. This was a big one. Although I had not seen Dr. Zlupko's TED Talk prior to my breakdown, I used similar strategies to work through this cycle, learn from the experience and move forward.

I am happy to say that, with extreme dedication and commitment, while spending several months away from home to work on himself, my son was able to turn things around. Ironically, so much of what he learned during this time away revolved around the principles in this book. I am grateful he had this opportunity to increase his awareness and cultivate his emotional intelligence. Sadly, for our children today, the traditional school curriculum is more focused on academics than practical life skills. A complete flaw in the structure of our education system if you ask me, but that's a topic for a whole new book!

Depending on the depth and breadth of your problem, one of the following strategies—or a combination thereof—will help you move forward through your stuckedness. Give these a try next time you are stuck.

Pick an adjective that is the opposite of what you are experiencing and focus on that adjective. For example, if you are experiencing a feeling of frustration because the snooze button on your alarm is getting the better of you, replace frustration with satisfaction then envision yourself jumping out of bed each morning when the alarm goes off. Allow yourself to experience the feeling of satisfaction that will come by getting out of bed right away and being ready to tackle your day.

Watch out for all-or-nothing polarized thinking. Nothing is absolute. For example, you may be thinking, *I'm the worst student in the world* –or– *I'm a horrible mom* –or– *I'm a terrible salesperson*. None of these things are ever true, and these thoughts serve no purpose. Thoughts that are highly polarized have the greatest power to manifest, which means the more we think this, the more likely it is to become true.

Recognize that what you are experiencing is a bump. It is not the be all and end all of your existence or who you are. View it as an opportunity to change and grow.

Do not let your ego get in the way. Yes, your problem is different and unique to you, but that does not mean that others have not tackled similar or worse problems and persevered. You can and will get past it.

Do not let fear take you down. Overcome the fear by recognizing the emotion and processing it, which is discussed further in Chapter 5.

Overcome your pride that tells you, "I don't need to learn" –or– "I'm doing everything right" –or– "It's everyone else's fault." Recognize that this pride is holding you back. If you were doing everything right, you wouldn't be stuck, and you would be able to work through the problem. If you're blaming others or circumstances for the situation, then shame on you for relinquishing the power of choice and putting your life in anyone else's hands.

Be persistent recognizing that persisting once is completely ineffective. Persistence by its very definition means "firm or obstinate continuance in a course of action in spite of difficulty or opposition". Do what it takes until the desired results are achieved. Persistence will help overcome the problem you thought was going to unhinge you.

Above all else, always commit to moving forward.

Some other things you can try include:

1. Break It Down—Sometimes the reason we get stuck is because the task at hand is just so overwhelming that we do not know where to start. The best thing to do in this case is to break down the project, instead of thinking about ways to accomplish the end game, work on the plays that are going to get you there.
2. Take a Break—There is a lot to be said for physical activity. Some of our best ideas and thoughts come to us when we are physically active. Leave your project, take a walk, go to the gym, for a run

or cycle. Whatever it is that gets you active and allows you an opportunity to clear your head. Quite often, this is all it may take for you to get back on track.

3. Collaborate—Often times, talking through your stuckedness will help the ideas flow again. Speaking with a colleague, mentor, or friend who may be able to offer some advice can help you find the answers.
4. Recognize the signs—You have blocked off two hours in your calendar to work on a project, but when the time allotted arrives, you deal with other more "pressing" things, making the excuse that they had to get done when, in fact, there was no need to interrupt your scheduled time at all. Then you put it off again. Procrastination is a key indicator of being stuck. In addition, stress and other physical or emotional symptoms can appear when you get into this mode. Know what these symptoms are. The earlier you can identify the signs, the quicker you can begin dealing with your stuckedness, and the sooner you will become unstuck. Do not make excuses, take action.
5. Gain a new perspective—Get comfortable with being stuck. Think of it as an opportunity to reflect, regroup, repurpose, and grow. There are lessons in everything we do. Reflect about what you have learned from being stuck and how you have grown from it. After gaining this new perspective, the next time you get stuck, think about how much easier it is for you to work through your stuckedness. You have identified the signs early on, you've used strategies to help move you forward, and you've grown from the experience. The more often we

overcome our problems and swiftly move forward, the less time we will spend being stuck.

Finally, there is no right or wrong amount of time to be stuck, but if you find yourself becoming someone you are not proud of, a version of yourself that is not your best you, this is a good indicator that you have been stuck too long and it's time to take immediate action.

<u>Challenge #7</u>

Think of a current situation in your life that is holding you back. Review the strategies above and identify which ones will help you move forward then apply them to your situation.

3

Passion Fruit

Love the life you live, live the life you love.

—Bob Marley

Desire, the root of all passion

Do we ever really know what we want? My dream was to become a psychologist. I find the inner workings of the mind fascinating and always felt my calling was to help others. Am I a practicing psychologist today? No. However, I do believe I have helped people over the years in other ways, at least, that is something many others have told me. I mention this because, as much as we may believe we are *destined* to do certain things, the world works in mysterious ways.

I did many things the hard way in life and did so from a very early age. I have no one to blame but myself for this. As a stubborn teenager who worked two or three jobs at a time throughout high school, I thought I knew best. My parents divorced when I was fifteen years old and shortly after, my father moved to the US for work. Of course, as a sixteen- and seventeen-year-old girl, I decided I did not like the rules at home, so I did what any stubborn know-it-all teenager would do and moved out.

I rented a room from a friend for a period of time, moved back home and rented the basement apartment from my mom for a short period of time, then moved back out on my own for good following that. Oh, if I only knew then what I know now. In any event, every action we take molds us into the beings we become, so although it may have been a difficult path (for both my poor mother and me) this experience is a part of me, and who I am, and I am a stronger person for it.

During this time, I worked in the restaurant/tavern-service industry, which was very lucrative for me. I decided to bypass college and university so I could continue earning money. I landed an office job at a paper manufacturing company as a customer service representative and continued to work part-time in the bar. Shortly after, the general manager offered me the office manager job, which of course, I accepted. After all, how many nineteen-year-old office managers do you know? It was a great job for a couple of years. I gained a lot of experience and travelled a couple of times a year to the head office in the US. Life should have been grand, but I felt like something was missing.

The year was 1992, I was twenty-two years old and making $32,000 a year, which was good money for my age—at least that is what my boss kept telling me. I could not help but think that I was underpaid and that if they just paid me what other office managers were making, I would be happy. My immediate boss and his boss were both male and both Americans. Although I did ask for a review of my salary on a couple of occasions, typically following a performance review which yielded a high rating, I was only ever given the standard 2 or 3 percent increase.

At the time, I did not know what the position was really worth, although I was quite certain it was worth more than what I was making. This was before the internet, so Google (which is now my best friend) could not help me. I wrote to Statistics Canada the old-fashioned way and spent some time in the library doing research. I found that the average salary range for my position was $38,000 to $46,000 per year. Armed with this information, I wrote a business case to my boss and *his* boss outlining my accomplishments, the average salary range for people within the same industry, and at the same level of position as me, and I requested they reconsider my request for increase.

Following a review of my request—and to my surprise—the company decided to raise my salary to $42,000 a year. I had received a $10,000 annual increase just like that! This was bound to make me happy! Certainly, this had to be the reason I did not feel fulfilled.

I was extremely grateful for the increase and their faith in me. I went on with my work only to find that, after a few short months, there was still something missing. Ugh. I felt that I had gone as far as I could go with that company. I was no longer learning and growing. I was not passionate about what I was doing. In the end, I realized it was not about the money at all, it was about desire and passion. Although grateful for their faith in me and the monetary increase they provided, it was time to move on, so I left this job, kept my part-time job bartending, and went back to school.

I share this story with you to demonstrate that money is not always the answer, and sometimes the problem is not what you think it is. You can have a good job or career and make great money, but if your work does not fulfill you, if you are not passionate about what you do day in and day out, whether it's a job or just life in general, then something will always be missing. Take some time to reflect on what makes you happy, what drives you, what makes you feel your best then try to incorporate more of that into your life.

I typically tend to gravitate towards doing things that do not make money. Volunteering for various associations, pro-bono teaching and training, you name it. If it is something you will not be getting paid for, sign me up! It got to a point that when I would be catching up with my dad on the phone, anytime I mentioned I was doing this or that the first thing he would ask me was whether I was getting paid for it. More often than not, the answer was no. If I could make money at finding things to do that do not pay you, I would be a multi-millionaire! However, it did not matter to me. I would always find a way to say yes to an opportunity if it aligned with my values, passions and goals.

One thing's for certain, if we do not have clear goals, then we do not know what we are working towards. Goals, dreams, thoughts, hope and action all guide us in the direction we want to go and help us live our extraordinary lives.

One… Two… Three… Let's Goal!

Do you ever feel like your life is on autopilot? Do you set ambitious goals only to find yourself a fraction of the way towards achieving them after many months? If you have answered yes to either of these questions, you are not alone. A study conducted by the University of Scranton[3] found that 92 percent of people do not achieve their goals!

A goal is the object of a person's ambition or desired result. In general, people will set goals to have an objective to work towards. Sometimes we meet those goals and other times, we do not. One thing is for certain, if we do not have a clear vision of what goals we want to achieve in life, we will certainly not be in a position to get there.

There have been many books, articles, and blogs written on how to set and obtain goals, most of which have a common message. Set goals that are SMART (specific, measurable, attainable, relevant, and time-bound) and goals that you are passionate about. After all, if you are not passionate about obtaining a goal, how are you ever going to be motivated to achieve it?

Let us take a closer look at what a SMART goal is:

- Specific
  When describing your goal, the more specific you are in relation to what you want to achieve, the easier it will be to identify a pathway to get there. For example, let's say you want to save money for a family vacation. Rather than just writing down *save for family vacation*, do some research into vacation destinations, determine how much money you will need to save to pay for it (including all the incidentals), then create a plan as to how you are going to get there, for example, *I am going to set up an automatic transfer with my bank so that $150 from each paycheck will be directly deposited into a savings account for the next 12 months*. A visual reminder or representation of what you are trying to achieve will also help to remind you what you are working towards—perhaps a picture of the destination, in this case, hanging in the kitchen for the family to see.

- Measurable
  When setting goals, we need to be sure that our progress can be measured. Determine at what intervals you will measure your progress towards your goals, for example, monthly, quarterly, etc. At each of these intervals, track where you are in relation to achieving your goal, revisit your strategy if necessary, and commit to moving forward with your plan. This is a perfect time to assess any obstacles you faced, how you dealt with them, and how you will handle them moving forward. You can assess, too, if any circumstances have changed, and if so, how they affect attaining your goal, if at all, and whether you can do more to achieve your goal than you had originally planned.

- Attainable
  Our goals should be challenging to keep us motivated but not overwhelming to the point we do not know where to start. As you may well know by now, I am a firm believer that we can achieve anything we *truly* want in life if we are passionate enough about it. That said, breaking down our goals into smaller chunks so they do not overwhelm us can be a good idea at times. Let us look at another example. Perhaps achieving an MBA is one of your goals. You do the research and immediately get dissuaded by the cost and time investment. You put it out of your mind because you feel that two years and $50,000 is unattainable. However, if you break it down, you will find that it is not so overwhelming. Take a look at the curriculum and cost and break it down by quarter. Determine which courses you would take in the first quarter and the associated cost, perhaps even do some research on available grants or loans to help with the cost. Take it quarter by quarter, and before you know it, the two years will have passed, you will have completed the MBA and that goal will have been achieved.

- Relevant
  This really speaks to your passion. If you are passionate about your goals, they will be relevant to who you want to be and how you want to show up in life. It is so easy to get distracted by "shiny object syndrome". We have access to so much at our fingertips, and sometimes find ourselves being pulled in a bunch of different directions. It happens to me all the time. I want to do so many different things, but there is only so much time (and money). When I catch myself wanting to sign up for this course or that certification or purchase one program or another, I take a step back and think

about how the purchase and time investment will help me in achieving the specific goals I have *already* set for myself. If there is no correlation, I choose to take a pass, for now. It does not mean that I will never take the course or program, it just means that it's not relevant at this exact moment in time.

- Time Bound
    Without a date to work towards, it will be difficult to find and sustain motivation. Not only that, if there is no time limit to achieving your goals, what will you measure, and how on earth will you ever be in a position to set new goals? Goal setting is all about growing ourselves. Growth should be a constant in our lives. If we are not growing, we are not learning, and if we are not learning, we become stagnant.

It is also important to remember that goals come in all sizes, shapes, and forms. They do not have to be big and life changing—small and life *shifting* are just as important. Making tiny shifts in the way you do things day to day will have a long-term positive effect on how you live your life and will play an integral role in achieving those bigger goals.

Before setting any goal—big, small, or otherwise—you will need to understand why you want to attain the goal. It is not enough just to want something; you need to know *why* you want it. Without understanding the why, you will not be able to develop the habits (behaviour) required to attain the goal. Remember, our beliefs drive our behaviour, and our behaviour feeds into our habits. The beliefs we have about our goals will help us develop the behaviours we require to attain them.

Finally, achieving goals is rewarding and increases our dopamine levels—dopamine being the feel-good chemical in our brain that we discussed earlier. So basically, when we set and achieve our goals, we are generally happier with ourselves, and in life, isn't this what it's all about?

Doug Bundock is a colleague and friend whom I admire and respect so very much. I love his outlook on life and his selfless desire to truly want to make a difference in the world and positively impact the lives of others. There are people in the world who try to portray the perception of altruism and then there are others in the world who truly live this life with their heart and soul. Doug is among the latter. I admire Doug for so many reasons and was very happy he agreed to share some insight with me that I could in turn share with you about what helps him live an extraordinary life day in and day out.

Earlier this year, Doug experienced some difficult times as his mother fell ill, and he experienced some loss of revenue, but he came through it realizing that life was going to be okay. Putting things into perspective was something that really helped Doug, and he has come through these difficult times feeling at peace through reflection and the realization that sometimes you have to set the reset button on life.

Goal setting is extremely important to Doug. He takes this very seriously and attributes his success in life to being regimented with his goals. He has a quarterly exercise wherein he sets his goals for the year in the first quarter, continually reviews them, notes benchmarks, and tweaks them where needed in the following quarters. If he is having a difficult day or needs a little nudge to get him out of a funk, he will reflect on his goals and take solace in the fact that he has direction and things to work towards.

He adds that it is important to write your goals down by hand, not on a computer. There are studies which suggest that by physically writing the goals, they become a part of your subconscious, and then the goal becomes more real and more a part of you. Sometimes he finds goals get accomplished on their own as they become by-products of other tasks. The mind is an amazing thing. Monthly review of the goal sheet is also very important. It keeps it all front and center.

Doug surrounds himself with good people and loves what he does. When faced with a difficult career decision, Doug reflected on his values, his goals, and the people around him to help guide him in his decision-making process. Intuition and persistence will help guide you through the path of life.

> ### Challenge #8
>
> Think of something that you want to achieve, it can be something small like getting more sleep at night or something big like making the honour roll or quitting smoking. Describe this goal and why you want to achieve it.
>
> Describe how you are going to achieve this goal and be specific.
>
> Identify an accountability partner, someone who you are going to share this goal with and who will help keep you on track through weekly, bi-weekly, or monthly communications.
>
> Once you have completed these three steps, write out your plan including specifics and timelines, contact your accountability partner to set the communication structure into place, and get started!

Remember, everyone falls off track. The important thing is to, first, forgive yourself (more on this in chapter 7) then identify the obstacles you faced, learn from them, and strategize around how to deal with those obstacles moving forward. One of my mentors, Paul Martinelli (President of the John Maxwell Team) suggests there are five steps to growth.

1. Test
2. Fail
3. Learn
4. Improve

5. Re-enter

Keep these steps in mind and faith in your heart as you work through your goals, and make sure your goals are aligned with what success means to you and who you are/want to be as a person.

Life's more fun in the sweet spot

Do what you love; love what you do.

People talk about work–life balance. I have never loved that phrase. Perhaps because I have generally loved what I do, so I do not consider work to be "work" in the traditional sense. To me, life is about being fluid. About doing things that are rewarding, doing things that are required of me, and doing what brings me my greatest returns. It is not about the money. It is not about the job. It is not about the house, the car, or the boat (not that I have a boat). It is about my life as a whole. Both tangibles and intangibles combined. It is about the experiences, the relationships, laughs, and the fun. It's about doing what you love to do most of the time and doing what you have to do only some of the time. Have I gone through phases in my life where I did not like what I was doing? Of course. I am sure we all have, but I like to live by the Pareto principle (the 80/20 rule) to keep me in check. If I can do what I love 80 percent of the time, then I can live with the 20 percent that does not necessarily put a bounce in my step.

Dr. Maxwell tells us that you should find something you love to do so much that you would do it for free and then do it so well people will pay you for it. Some people think it is the other way around—pay me enough, and I will be happy. However, you can never make a person that is unhappy happy by giving them more of the same thing.

I read an *Inc.* magazine article by Steve Farber where he shares the mantra:

> "Do what you love in the service of people who love what you do."

Wow. Such great wisdom, and it goes to support the philosophy that when we do what we love, we will do it so well that people will demand it from us.

Not only do you stand to make more money by doing what you love, researchers are now finding a strong connection between longevity and work. In an eight-decade study, led by Dr. Howard S. Freidman coined the "Longevity Project," researchers found that, among other things, men and women who were continually productive were healthier and lived longer than their less-driven peers. Work is an essential ingredient for a happy life, and now research suggests that working hard in a field you love will give your life meaning and purpose. Productive work, whether paid or volunteer, keeps you active and challenges you to continue learning and to be your best self.

There was a twenty-year study (and I must admit, I cannot recall the source though I remember the details) of 1,500 people who were split into two groups, Group A and Group B. The people of Group A chose to do a job solely for the purpose of making money so they could enjoy life later. The people in Group B chose to pursue what they loved to do so they could enjoy life now. One hundred and one of those 1,500 people became millionaires. All but one of the millionaires came from Group B. So you see, even the science tells us that when you do what you love, you have a higher chance of being successful (whatever that looks like for you).

One of the keynote presentations I do is on "Aligning Your Why". It focuses on individuals aligning their passions and values with those of the organization they work with and directs organizations to create a culture conducive to aligning with the passions and values of their employees.

In the presentation, I take the audience through a bit of a journey to get them thinking about their *why*, their passions and their purpose. Knowing our *why* gives us freedom, builds our confidence, and makes an impact on others. Believing in it gives us longevity and purpose.

Discovering your *why* or your purpose in life is an intensive process. Some of you may have already engaged in the process and know your *why*; for others, this may be a brand-new concept. You have to ask yourself many questions, and in the end, you still must figure out a way for your why to impact what you do.

Often times, we must lose ourselves to find ourselves, forgetting what we *think* we know and focusing on who we are and what makes us tick. Our *why* creates security and comfort for you in everything you do. There is a deep connection between your strengths and your *why*. The more you work out of your strength zone in pursuit of your *why*, the more you increase both. Your *why* is your motivation to make every day count, no matter your age. It provides you with the necessary fuel to live until you die.

Although I have only been able to articulate my *why*—or purpose, if you prefer—for a few years now, the crux of it has been a part of me throughout my life. I have always enjoyed serving others. In my early childhood I played host to my mom and her friends, serving them coffee and treats, then in my part time jobs as a waitress or bartender serving food or drinks to patrons to dinner parties for friends in my home or serving struggling youth at the Yonge Street Mission in Toronto. Helping people see the best in themselves, encouraging them to believe in themselves, and serving them to contribute to their happiness are some of the things that make my heart sing. When you look at the things that made you happy over your lifetime, you will begin to visualize your purpose. I was able to articulate my why only after doing some intense work which included a lot of introspection and retrospection. It goes something like this:

> *I want to make a difference. I want to help people be the best possible version of themselves they can be. I will encourage people to believe in themselves and value their purpose. I will help them understand that their destiny is within their control and that dreams can become reality. I will empower people of all ages to strive to achieve self-actualization, to enlighten them so they understand the world is at their fingertips and that they can do whatever they set out to do. I will foster the mantra "positive thinking leads to positive results". I will encourage people to create and celebrate awesomeness wherever they find it so that in time, they will find more of it within themselves. I will help them be intentional in their journey to live an extraordinary life.*

Our *why* may evolve over the years, and our *what* (what you do) will certainly change, but the core will always remain the same.

Challenge #9

Let us take some time to identify your strengths, your passions, and your greatest joy because inevitably, your version of success will be incumbent upon infusing more of these things into your daily life and being able to articulate your *why*.

I want you to identify a safe space in your world and commit to spending thirty to sixty minutes in this space to start thinking about what inspires you and what makes you your best you. Ask yourself the following questions:

What are my top five strengths? What am I really good at?

What do I feel very deeply about? What do I love?

What brings me my greatest joy? When am I happiest?

What does *"being at my best"* –or– *"a successful life"* look like for me?

4

Flip the Negative Switch to Off

Protect your enthusiasm from the negativity of others.

—H. Jackson Brown Jr.

Attitude

Your attitude is yours and yours alone. Don't ever let someone else hijack it! If someone is in a bad mood or in a negative space, do not let them bring you down. Attitudes are infectious both ways, good and bad. Let the good attitude seep on in, and shut the door before the bad attitude can get its foot wedged in there.

In 2016, I was in Paraguay along with approximately 200 other coaches from the John Maxwell Team. We were invited by the country's president to train the leaders of the seven streams of influence on leadership. We trained approximately 20,000 leaders by the time we had left, and these leaders would train a further 700,000 Paraguayans by the end of the year. Each day was brand new experience. We were never in the same place twice.

On one of the days, I was fortunate enough to end up at Congress. During one of the round table sessions with some congressional representatives and diplomats, we were discussing the value of attitude and how it plays an integral role in leadership and life. When we got to the part about what each person could do to improve their attitude, I used the example of saying good morning to people as you walk into the office each day. One of the congresswomen, speaking through an interpreter, said that she had tried that once, and people looked at her as if she was crazy, so she never did it again. I asked her what she thought would happen if she tried again and her colleague beside her did the same thing and then again every day for a week. Before long, people would consider this the norm and would be looking at anyone who did not say good morning as crazy. It was a lightbulb moment for the whole room as everyone started to nod their heads in agreement.

My point being, attitude is infectious. We can create a positive environment with a good attitude or a negative environment with a poor attitude.

That being said, attitude is about more than just being positive or negative, it is how we look at life and about how we show up every day. These things ultimately drive the results we see in our lives. A poor attitude will result in a less than stellar life, and a stellar attitude will result in an extraordinary life.

We discussed the power of choice earlier on. This comes into play here as well, with our attitude. Our attitude about things that happen in our lives or about the circumstances in which we currently live have a huge impact on how we feel day to day. Think about some of the circumstances in your life right now that are less than great, now think about your attitude towards these things. Is that attitude healthy and is it serving you—or does it only bring you down?

I will demonstrate with an example. I love what I do. I love almost everything about it, but I have a long commute to and from the city each day. If I allowed this to get me down, I would stress over that drive every day. This stress would manifest inside to the point I would most likely start hating my job or walk around as a big old stress ball. This would inevitably lead to me having a more negative outlook on life, which would then most likely cause me to be miserable and project that misery on my children and/or the people closest to me. That would stink, for everyone! Instead, I choose to take the attitude that this time on the road is time to catch up with my friends and family on the phone (hands free of course) and listen to podcasts so I can continue to grow and develop myself as a person. Now, I am not going to lie to you and say I love spending so much time on the road, but I can honestly say that my attitude toward it has saved me from a version of myself that I have no interest being.

A number of factors including our emotional state of mind at any given time can drive our attitude. In order to understand our emotions a little better, it helps to know a little bit about the amygdala, a brain structure considered to be part of our limbic system. The amygdala stimulates emotional recall and responses and is a significant contributor to the nucleus accumbens—a brain structure that is part of our pleasure and reward system and activates our motivation, allowing willpower to translate into action. Now, this is not a book on psychology, biology, or neuroscience, so I will not bore you with any more details about the anatomy of the brain, but in order to be our best selves, we should really be familiar with these parts of our brain and how they work so we can manipulate them for the greater good!

Research suggests that when the left side of the amygdala is stimulated, people experience happiness and are more optimistic which leads them to be more focused on opportunities over challenges because of the positive thoughts that are triggered. This drives people to action and ultimately helps them to achieve their goals thereby creating happy experiences and generating positive feedback.

When the right side of the amygdala is stimulated, people tend to experience fear-based reactions releasing adrenalin and cortisol into the bloodstream, which makes us, feel anxious, fearful, or edgy. In a nutshell, the amygdala forms associations with stimuli, which trigger a positive or negative response.

That's all fine and dandy, but how do we control which part of our amygdala is being stimulated. Well, technically, you cannot control this at source, but you can manipulate it. We must recognize the stimuli for what it is—just a trigger—and change how we think about it. Let us look at an example. Say in your younger years you spent some time getting into trouble at home and the repercussions always involved the words "wait until your father gets home". Inevitably, when you heard the front door close, fear would immediately set in, in anticipation of what was to come. Your brain continues to associate a door closing with fear throughout your life. Until we develop awareness about the fact this is an isolated or outdated response to the stimuli, we cannot change it.

Being aware allows us to stop, understand the emotion for what it is, process it to determine what triggered it, and then replace it with a new emotion. Perhaps you choose to replace the emotion of fear with that of opportunity so the next time you hear a door close, the left side of your amygdala is triggered, and you feel excited about the possibilities before you.

Challenge #10

Step 1.

Describe a circumstance in your life that is not the best, something you would like to change and your attitude about it.

Step 2.

Think about your attitude towards this situation and what it would look like if you changed your attitude to a more positive one. Describe what this looks like.

Step 3.

Commit to changing your attitude about this one thing every day for the next 30 days. You can even go as so far to set an alarm each morning to remind you about it. Watch what happens at the end of those 30 days. I bet you will feel emotionally and physically lighter after replacing the poor attitude with a better one!

Describe how changing your attitude for 30 days affected your outlook on the situation.

—

Words Are a Powerful Thing

Positive affirmation is a powerful tool. Studies have shown that what we are told (or what we tell *ourselves*) drives our beliefs, and our beliefs drive our behaviour. Children who are constantly told they are useless, a disappointment, or a failure more often than not grow up believing that is what they are so there is no point in trying to achieve anything better. The good news is that these negative forces can be overcome! I introduced you to your amygdala in the previous excerpt; well it comes into play here as well. Remember I talked about how the amygdala also stimulated the reward part of the brain? Well that happens through the use of positive words either when someone else speaks them or it can be your own self-talk.

I play in a ladies' golf league in the summer. I have met some wonderful women along the way, and we always have fun, despite how we may golf sometimes! However, it never fails, inevitably at least once during the round, one of the women will say something to the effect, "I can never get the ball up that hill" – or– "I'm swapping my ball for an older one because I always end up in the water here." I am sure many of you who have played golf have uttered those words at one point or another, myself included! It was not until I really started studying the power of mindset that I began to change my thinking and therefore my words. In fact, Bobby Jones says, "Golf is played on a 5-inch course—the distance between your ears."

Golf, much like life, is all in your head. When we tell ourselves that we are going to make the shot and we visualize the ball falling where we want it to land, it is more likely to get there. Now, I am not a great golfer, nor would I ever give anyone advice on how to play the game, I reserve that for the experts. But what I will say is that when I play a game using visualization, positive words to describe the shot I am about to make, and when I accept poor shots as ones of isolation as opposed to an indication of how my whole game will go, my game drastically improves.

It is no different when something goes wrong in the morning and your natural instinct is to say, "it's going to be one of those days." These words just set us up for failure. One day, I had a significant presentation to make in front of some very senior leaders. For some reason, I woke up a little later than typical that morning so as I ran to jump in the shower, I stubbed my toe. Not a huge issue—it was sore, but I could still squeeze it into a pair of heels. After getting dressed, I proceeded to make my morning smoothie. When I went to remove the canister from the smoothie maker, the lid remained on the base causing a very berry smoothie to fly all over the kitchen cabinets, floor and of course the outfit that I had strategically selected the night before. After spewing a few choice words, I cleaned the kitchen and myself up and went on my way, sans smoothie.

Now, these things could have sent my day for a loop if I chose to let them. I could have very easily told myself "it was going to be one of those days," which would have put me in a poor state of mind leading to a less-than-my-best version of myself showing up at this very important presentation. Instead, I chose to let it roll off. I vowed to stop hitting the snooze button, chuckled at my clumsiness, and made a mental note to always double twist the smoothie maker in the opposite direction before removing it from the blender thingy. I considered myself lucky that I did not way over sleep, break my toe, or slice my finger on the blade, and was grateful for the opportunity to give a presentation that day. Guess what, it did not turn out to be "one of those days" at all. The feedback on the presentation was awesome, I did not lose my toe, and my smoothie maker lived to make smoothies another day.

In his book, *The Power of Positive Thinking*, Noman Vincent Peale tells us a story about a couple he met on a train. The wife was quite unpleasant and complained about everything from her surroundings to the service and food. Her husband was genial, affable, and easy going. When Peale asked what business they were in, he responded by saying he was a lawyer and his wife was in the manufacturing business. Peale asked what kind of manufacturing and the response was "unhappiness—she manufactures her own unhappiness."

Our state of mind is exactly how we choose it to be. If we infiltrate it with negative thoughts, resentment, ill-will, and hate, it is impossible to have an optimistic outlook on life, and without a positive outlook how can you ever enjoy an extraordinary life? (After all, there will always be *something* wrong.)

In his book *Intentional Living*, John Maxwell says, "there is a difference between having good intentions and living intentionally." There are words we use that he describes as words of good intention such as "I wish" –and– "someday" –and– "hopefully" and then there are words that are used when living your life with intention such as "I will" –and– "today" –and– "definitely". Notice the difference. When we speak using words of definite action, we will start to be more intentional in our lives.

Of course, this can be easier said than done and takes specific discipline. You will need to think about your words before you speak them. If it were as hard to say things as it is to do things, we wouldn't say a word. The more we say the right things and tell ourselves that this is how life is to be, the more it will be. How many times have we said we were going to do something and not do it? However, how many times have we ever done something without actually saying it first? Words are a powerful thing.

Challenge #11

Think back to a time when you said something to the effect of: "It's going to be one of those days." Describe what you could have done differently to affect the outcome of that day.

Describe a recent situation where you used words of good intentions, and then think of how you could change those words to make them more intentional. For example: Instead of saying, "I wish I could get out of bed when the alarm goes off instead of always hitting the snooze button," try saying, "I am going to feel so good about getting a jump on my day by getting out of bed when the alarm goes off."

Spend Time with Lifters, Not Anchors

As a child or even an adult, how many times have you been told to stop daydreaming? Stop daydreaming and do your work. In other words, stop thinking about how things could be and get back to the work that you have to do to make money. Stop creating dreams and possibilities and get back to your life because you cannot change it anyway. Such ignorance. Ignorance because the people saying these things are ignorant to possibility. They choose to believe that they have very little control over their own lives and must take things at face value, which is the complete opposite of the truth.

Who are you spending your time with? Are they people who lift you up or pull you down like an anchor? Are they telling you to stop dreaming or to dream big? Of course, we need all types of people in our lives, but too many anchors and not enough lifters will certainly bring us down.

We all have individuals in our circle that either elevate our mood or deflate it. Sometimes we need to do a health check to ensure we are spending time with those who are good for our mental well-being. I am not talking about discarding a friend or family member if they are going through a rough time. Of course, we need to be there for them as they are for us in our times of need. I am talking about the life-long Eeyores of the world who continually walk around with the grey cloud over their heads and refuse to see the good in others and in themselves.

You have heard the saying "you are what you eat," well in applying this to your inner circle; one might say you are who you spend your time with. It is a fact that you begin to think like the people who you spend the most time with. If your positivity is not rubbing off on them, it may be time to move on before their negativity rubs off on you. Not only do you risk becoming more negative yourself, it is emotionally draining to spend time with someone who is in a constant negative state. Have you ever noticed the difference in your energy after spending a half an hour speaking with someone who is upbeat, positive, and generally enjoyable to be around as opposed to spending the same amount of time with someone who complains the whole conversation about anything from family to work or life? In the former, you leave that conversation energized, perhaps even inspired. With the latter, you leave feeling drained and exhausted, possibly not even wanting to engage in any further discussions with anyone else.

In her book, *No One Understands You and What To Do About It*, Heidi Grant Halvorson discusses the various lenses that people see you through. In her chapter on seekers and risk-mitigators, she discusses the differences between people who see things through a promotion lens vs. those that see things through a prevention lens. In a nutshell, promotion-lens-focused people are constantly seeking ways to be better. They seek opportunities and embrace risk. Prevention-lens-focused people are trying to hang on to what they already have, and are trying to keep things running smoothly. They are calculated and cautious. They plan effectively and are always prepared. There is no right or wrong here, just different perspectives. Typically, the prevention-lens-focused individuals will be the ones who may not support the promotion-lens-focused people in their desire to be more, grow more, and do more. What is important to understand here is that the perceived lack of understanding on why you want to do something is about the person who has the lack of understanding, not about you as a person.

I previously mentioned my Paraguay journey with the John Maxwell team. This was a volunteer mission, so I had to pay my way which I had no hesitation doing. The growth I would experience on this journey would be invaluable. To be able to add value to so many people and play an integral role in transforming a country was truly an opportunity of a lifetime and a no-brainer for me. I was obviously very excited about this. On a telephone call to one of my inner circle, I had mentioned that I had just gone to get my inoculations for the trip and I was ready to go! The comment in response was; why in the world would I want to do this? I thought, *why on Earth wouldn't I?*

It is comments like these, which people make on a regular basis, that continually remind me we are not all the same, which of course is not a bad thing, just different.

In an *Inc.* magazine article written by Peter Economy[4], he suggests it is not only about banishing toxic people in our life, we need to keep the right people in our life as well. For him, that means a leader, a listener, a storyteller, the happy one, and the one who forces you to think. I tend to agree, especially about the person who forces you to think because, let's face it, if you are the smartest one in the room, you are in the wrong room! Just remember, although a mix of difference is good, we have to be sure it is not anchoring us down.

On this trip to Paraguay, I met an amazing woman by the name of Louise Elliott. The story of how we met is an interesting one, which I will save for later. The moment we met, I knew there was something very special about her. She exuded a confidence combined with humility that is a very distinct and rare feature. Louise lives in Columbus, Ohio, is the mother of a very successful teenage son, a senior executive, an entrepreneur and the author of *The BrainPower Pyramid: 7 proven steps for how to Sleep like a Baby, Run like a Cheetah, Fuel like a Formula One Car, Create like Edison, Think like Da Vinci, Learn like Einstein And Network like a Rockstar!* I highly recommend you read her masterpiece!

Louise and I really hit it off on this trip, kept in touch, and spent some time together at conference the following year. It was clear from the moment we met that she had a great outlook on life and was someone I would want to be in my inner circle. When I asked her if she would contribute to this book, she responded with a grateful and gracious yes—she was happy to help because that is the type of person Louise is.

One of the things Louise explained to me is that in her quest to be her best self, she tries to surround herself with happiness and positivity and this includes her clients. If she is coaching a client that has a perpetual black cloud over them every time they meet, she will remind them that they are on a journey together and in order to make the most of the journey, people need to be at a point in their life where they are accepting of the help. She works with people to help them find things that feed their soul and identify why they are doing what they are doing and how to change habits to fulfil themselves. One of the obstacles she faces is when people are not willing to make the leap. If they are not willing and continue to bring the cloud with them, she will respectfully let them know that it is probably best they move forward on their own and will disengage from the relationship.

She views her personal relationships in the same light. Louise had a lot of toxicity around her in her work, marriage, and family life at one point, none of which was serving her or feeding her soul. Misery loves company, so if you choose to continue living in a toxic environment, you too will become toxic. She says when negativity enters her life, she will assess whether she needs to fix it or exit it. You have to make the tough decisions so as not to be caught up in the pattern of negativity.

Louise focuses on living her best life, and to her, that means recognizing what she was put on this earth to do and understanding what fulfils her. She gives herself a daily reminder to help people. To be able to help people turn their lives around, influence others in their life path, and have the opportunity to change someone's life for the better are the things Louise is passionate about. She shares that while you cannot always follow people in their journey; fulfillment will come from knowing she has left an imprint on their life. Her words of advice: Always do things that make your heart sing.

We all see things through different lenses. What is important to some is not to others, and how some people see things is completely different from how others perceive them to be. There is no right or wrong here. People's perspectives will differ based on a variety of things, and so what is enjoyable to some will be like getting teeth pulled for others. That said, we cannot let those who see things through a different lens impact the choices we make because of it.

Next time someone questions why you would want to venture outside of your comfort zone to try something new—suggesting that perhaps you are too old or not smart enough and why not leave well enough alone—think about the source of the discouragement and consider the successes or lack thereof of the naysayer. Most often, people who stifle the goals or dreams of others are ones who lack the ambition, drive, and courage to challenge themselves. Therefore, they are not as likely to support others in their desires. In contrast, successful, happy people want to see others succeed and will do everything they can to support you. Think about the source of discouragement then talk yourself through accordingly.

There are many benefits to spending time with people who encourage, uplift, support, and cheer for you, not against you, some of which include improved health, reduced stress, and increased creativity. Lifters genuinely want to see you do well.

We all deserve happiness, success, and abundance in our lives. In his book *Think and Grow Rich*, Napoleon Hill says it perfectly:

Success comes to those who become success conscious. Failure comes to those who indifferently allow themselves to become failure conscious.[5]

Challenge #12:

Describe a time someone discouraged you from doing something and your reaction:

The next time someone discourages you from doing something, describe how will you handle it?

5

Who am I today?

*When you change the way you look at things.
The things you look at change.*

—*Wayne Dyer*

Be Present in the Moment

Sometimes we get so wrapped up in where we want to go that we forget to enjoy where we are. It is like when you are young, you cannot wait to be older, and as you get older, sometimes you wish you were younger.

What if we lived as if we were present every day, enjoyed each moment of every minute, and truly experienced every emotion that ran through our soul? It is a beautiful way to experience life.

New York is one of the kids' and my favourite places to visit in the United States. When my daughter was in Grade 12, she asked if we could go to NYC to prom dress shop. I packaged it as her Christmas gift and she, her best friend, and my mom and stepdad, Bill, made a weekend of it. It was December 2015, and we were experiencing an unseasonably warm winter that year, as was New York.

On one of the days, we decided to go to Central Park and the Museum of Natural History. If you have ever spent any time in Central Park, you know how easy it is to get lost or turned around! About an hour or so into the park visit, we were anxious to find the 81st Street exit so we could get to the museum. Now when I say "we", I really mean Bill and me. You see, I am a Type A personality and Bill being a retired police officer, Regional Counsellor, and successful real estate agent, is always go, go, go. It almost became like a little challenge to see which of us could find the exit first. After what seemed like forever, we were excited when we finally found the right exit! When I turned around to tell the girls (my daughter, her friend, and my mom), they were nowhere to be found. At some point, we had lost them in our haste to find the exit.

In a bit of a huff, shaking my head at the fact they had not kept up, I started to back track to find them while Bill manned the exit so we did not lose it again. I came upon them about ten minutes back, huddled around a garden. I waved at them. "Come on, we found the exit." My mom said, "Sorry, we just stopped to smell the roses. It's a thing you know."

Those words stopped me in my tracks. At first, I chuckled a little because, of course, I knew stopping to smell the roses was a saying and then I felt this amazing sense of awe come over me. I could not believe how ignorant I had been to the miracle of flowers blooming in the city in the middle of December on a ground that should have been covered with snow. How often would anyone get to experience that? Bill and I were so consumed with trying to find the exit of the park and check the next thing off our list that we completely lost site of the beautiful gift that was right before us.

From that day forward, I vowed to enjoy every experience and savour each moment. Now, this does not mean that I have not driven to work on autopilot here and there or looked back and wondered where the day/week/month has gone, but it really has given me a different perspective on life. I used to think time was going by quicker and quicker the older I got. I still believe that to some extent; however, I can honestly say that being present in the moment and truly experiencing each part of every day makes the time go just a little bit slower. Slower in a good way, not slower in a running-on- a-treadmill-wondering-if-you're-ever-going-to-get-to-thirty-minutes kind of way.

Along with being present, there is no point in dwelling on the past or worrying too much about the future. My father, who in his words has the perfect life, lives by this philosophy unconditionally. He has lived a very colourful life as an engineer in the production world and the vice president of Miss Universe Productions. He has travelled the world extensively and has many stories involving Russian diplomats, Billy Graham Crusades, several of the world Olympics, sporting events, concerts, and of course all the pageants, just to name a few. I have been begging him to start voice recording his stories so I can get to work on his biography. What an entertaining book that will be! However, I digress.

I included my dad in this book not for all that he has experienced or accomplished but because of how he lives his life. He loves his life and says each new day is filled with all sorts of potential. He attributes this love of life, at least in part, to not letting negative people in it and also to the fact that he never looks back. He says you cannot fix what happened yesterday and cannot worry about what is going to happen tomorrow.

He recently retired (although he still works contract simply because he loves what he does) and spends most weekdays day trading in the stock market. He says if he loses in the market one day, he does not dwell on that. He sets specific parameters about what he is willing to lose so if it goes, it goes. He has no regrets in life because he cannot change anything that has happened in the past, he can only move forward. He cannot control what happened one minute ago, only what is going to happen in the next. My dad will say that he is a very lucky man because has been blessed with a job that he loves and never has a bad day. These things are true, but I would add that it was my dad's desire that drove him to succeed, and by working in his sweet spot in a field he is passionate about and spending his days, retired or not, doing what he loves, he is living his extraordinary life day in and day out.

My brother and I recently went to visit my dad in Florida. On the way there, my brother was telling me about our family coat of arms and reminded me of the crest that used to hang in our grandparents' house. I recall seeing the griffin as a child, but at the time did not realize the meaning of it. The three of us were having a conversation about this during our visit. We learned so much about the Kip family coat of arms and our heritage, but the one thing that really stood out was the meaning associated with it. "Vestigia Nulla Retrorsum" is the Latin motto that surround our crest. The literal translation is "never a backwards step". Wow. What a powerful revelation this was for us because, without even knowing it, the three of us had been living our lives according to that motto. No backwards steps, never look back, do not dwell on the past, and only move forward. The Kip coat of arms and motto that I have been taught to live by my whole life.

Mindfulness

According to a *Harvard Gazette* article entitled "Wandering mind not a happy mind"[6], research conducted by psychologists Matthew A. Killingsworth and Daniel T. Gilbert of Harvard University found that people spent nearly half their time (46.9%) thinking about something other than what they are doing. Mindfulness is the practice of being present in the moment. Often when people hear the word mindfulness, they relate it to yoga and/or meditation. Although mindfulness is at the core of these things, you do not have to meditate or practice yoga to be mindful or present. The art of being present is simply bringing all of your awareness and attention to the moment you are in. Notice your surroundings, experience your feelings, and focus on the task at hand. When we are mindful, we are more in tune with our thoughts, emotions, and body sensations.

To be fully present takes work. Our brains naturally want to share so many things with us at any given time, but it is not our brain's fault: We are consistently told we need to multitask. We check multiple social media sites at one time. We are cooking dinner while entertaining the children. We are studying for an exam while listening to media and updating our snapchat story. Our poor brains do not have a chance! Unless of course, we are willing to give it one.

There are so many benefits to practicing mindfulness and being present. In fact, studies suggest that those who tend to live in the moment are happier, calmer, more relaxed and appreciative. They are more focused, even when not practicing mindfulness and less stressed. In addition, researchers have found that the simple act of practicing mindfulness increases both brain activity and brain tissue.

I have been practicing mindfulness for a number of years now. It is easy to get caught up in the crazy of life sometimes, but when I feel that happening, I will stop, take a few deep breaths, and bring my awareness back to the present moment. This tends to work well for me, to the point I do not have to think about being present most times—I just am.

This came to light recently in a work situation. Most days, the work I do requires me to be in back to back meetings. Following one of these meetings, a colleague of mine made a comment to me.

"I do not know how you do it Tammie," he said. "You go from one meeting to the next, and you are always so calm and prepared.

I do not understand it, I always feel so flustered no matter how much I have prepared."

Now, the person who made this comment to me is a project manager, so his job is literally running meetings for numerous projects. He is in just as many meetings as I am, if not more, on any given day.

I reflected on what he had said after I got home that evening, and it occurred to me that I am not any more prepared than he is for these meetings. In fact, often times I am reviewing the material just minutes before or if I am running the meeting, sometimes I have finished preparing the material just prior to the meeting. (Let's keep that one between us). I was no more prepared than he was; the difference was that I was present at every meeting. Not just my physical self, but emotionally and intellectually invested in each and every meeting. I do not think about the task list that came out of the prior meeting or worry about presenting at the next. I go into a meeting, fully aware and present because at that exact moment in time, this is where I need to be.

The beautiful thing about being present is that it applies to everything in life. Think of a world where you cherish every moment you have and savour each and every emotion that transcends through you, a world where you can clear your mind of the clutter and simply focus on what is before you. What an extraordinary world this is.

> ### Challenge #13
>
> Being present in the moment means truly experiencing everything associated with that moment. Choose a moment to practice this in the next twenty-four hours and describe the moment in your workbook. Be sure to include everything about the moment such as sounds, smell, who you were with, surroundings, emotions and thoughts provoked.

Sweet emotion

Someone once said to me "my career does not define me." She explained to me that she was happy to do a job that she liked, not necessarily loved, because she found her greatest rewards and treasures laid outside the walls of her career. This made sense to me, but it got me to thinking, there are other ways people can—and do—interpret this comment. Do your duties, title, place of employment or hierarchy in life define you? I would have to say the answer to that is no—although some people may challenge me on that. Then I took this one-step further and asked the question, does your position in your career/life define you, or do you define it? I think we have been together long enough now for you to know where I am going with this. Of course, we are the captains of our own ships and define our own lives. In order to do that, to be our best selves and define a life that makes us feel fulfilled and successful, we need to know where to start, and I cannot think of a better place to start than with awareness.

The results we have in life are always based on our current level of awareness. Increase your awareness, increase your results.

Simple right? If we are thinking, reading, and reflecting daily, we are increasing our emotional intelligence and in turn our level of awareness. It is a beautiful thing. As we become more aware of our emotions, the effect of our emotions on others and ourselves and are intentional in the decisions we make as well as the trickle effect of those decisions, we exist at a completely new level of being.

There is one slight side effect to this. As you continue to develop your awareness, you will continue to evolve and grow at a rate that will outpace others around you that are not necessarily developing their levels of awareness and emotional intelligence.

Although I only formally started studying the philosophy of leadership and mindfulness in 2014, I have always been a growth-conscious person, forever learning new things and seeking innovative opportunities. Because of this, I experienced said side effect above. I met who I thought was the love of my life in 1993. I was twenty-three years old. We fell madly in love and married three years later. My husband was ten years older than I was. We had two beautiful children together and lived a wonderfully happy life for about ten to twelve years. Then something changed. You see, I had experienced and grown so much over those years. I had gone back to school (again), had significantly advanced in my career, and had an insatiable desire to continually do more, learn more, and be more. Before I knew it, my husband and I had completely grown apart. He was still the sweet wonderful man I had fallen madly in love with, but I was a completely different person, operating at a new level of awareness that was not conducive to the relationship that was at the foundation of our marriage.

Now, I am not suggesting that you are going to grow apart from your spouse, friends, or family when you start working on yourself. That is not an absolute. What is absolute is that, by growing yourself and increasing your level of awareness and emotional intelligence, how you see life and others will change. How you show up today will be different from how you showed up yesterday, and how you show up tomorrow will be different from today.

To increase our self-awareness, we must reflect on the things we do well, identify our shortcomings and limitations, and begin to understand the things we do not know about ourselves.

One of my mentors always says, things must change *in* you for things to change *for* you. Sheer brilliance. So often people look for circumstances or people to change, laying blame on one thing or another when, in fact, our reaction to circumstance is what drives the results we experience. Once we become aware of this, our reactions will change, thereby changing our results. It goes back to the power of choice.

When we make decisions and choices from a heightened level of awareness, we are more apt to take a chance, venture into the unknown, do it afraid, and be confident in our decisions. Once we make our decisions, we need to be aware that there could be unpredicted implications to our emotions that we may not have thought of. It is important to recognize these emotions as they arise and process them accordingly.

I shared the story of my marriage with you earlier. Unfortunately, we had fallen apart, and I knew I had a decision to make. Did I sacrifice my happiness, enjoyment of life, and the ability to be my best me to raise my children in a loveless home, or did I make the break so we could all move on and start to build a new norm. Every situation is different. One choice is no better than the other is, and there are no right or wrong answers. In this particular situation, I decided it was best for me and my family to move on. Although I was confident in my decision, it took me years to process the feelings of guilt. In fact, I had not realized that I was still carrying those feelings until over six years later when they appeared in a hypnosis session.

I had started to experience little heart palpitations. The phenomenon was foreign to me. I thought I might be having some heart issues, so I went to the doctor. She ran a number of tests and confirmed, thankfully, that nothing was wrong with my heart. She attributed the palpitations to stress and/or anxiety, which was not surprising since this was around the time I was winding down the business and going through the struggles with my son. She suggested I continue to do what I was doing with yoga and meditation; however, the frequency of these palpitations continued to increase.

As you know, hypnosis had helped me in the past, so I decided to give it another shot. During my first appointment, I explained the physical experience my body was going through. My hypnotherapist took me on a journey into the past in three separate sessions, which allowed me to process unresolved feelings of guilt and failure related to my marriage. Although I was confident in my decision to leave the marriage, I was not reflecting on things much back then. The marriage ended, and I moved on—or so I had thought. I did this by diving into work, volunteering with the kids' sports and involving myself with industry causes. I did not take time to process all of the emotions that inevitably come along with the end of a relationship. It does not matter whether the end is because of death, divorce, or disassociation. Every relationship of some significance in our life needs to be mourned when it is over. This anxiety manifested over the years without any outward signs, but each time something happened that left me with a feeling of guilt or failure, the feelings would deepen and compound. It could be something as simple as inadvertently cutting someone off on the highway. The guilt would overwhelm me. Now obviously, cutting someone off on the highway is nothing to feel guilty over, but when you already carry around a lot of *unprocessed* guilt, even small incremental increases can be a lot to bear, and so something that another person might easily shrug off takes on the crushing weight of a felony.

As funny as this may sound, I am grateful that I experienced the physical manifestation of anxiety because it led me back to hypnosis, which taught me how to effectively process my feelings. Now, if something has happened and evokes emotions of anger, sadness or guilt, I follow this quick little guide.

1. I acknowledge the emotion and determine what it is that I'm feeling (angry, sad, guilty)
2. Identify what triggered the emotion
3. Rationalize my reaction to the emotion
4. Give myself some time to constructively express the emotion
5. Move on

Each of the steps are important. Most people want to go from step one straight to five, but trust me, if you skip out on steps two to four, you may find yourself sitting in the emergency room thinking your anxiety palpitations are a heart attack! Unprocessed or unresolved emotions are a powerful thing.

Our emotions tie into our self-awareness, which is one of the four components of emotional intelligence (EI). Emotional intelligence refers to a person's innate potential, the ability for someone to understand his or her own emotions as well as the emotions of others. Emotional quotient (EQ) is the scale used to measure emotional intelligence, just like IQ is the scale used to measure people's intellectual intelligence.

The four components of EI are self-awareness, self-management, social awareness, and relationship management. For purposes of this book, we will focus on self-awareness.

Self-awareness is the ability to accurately perceive your own emotions. People with high self-awareness are very clear on what they do well, what motivates them, and what pushes their buttons. As a person's self-awareness increases, so does their satisfaction with life and their ability to achieve their goals. When you are self-aware, you are far more likely to pursue the right opportunities, put your strengths to work, and keep emotions from holding you back by recognizing them—and how they affect you—and processing them properly rather than allowing them to control the situation.

It has been more than two decades since research first linked aspects of emotional intelligence to results. In a 1998 study, which continues to be referred to by experts today, conducted by the late David McClelland, a noted Harvard University psychologist, he found that leaders with strengths in a critical mass of six or more emotional intelligence competencies were far more effective than peers who lacked such strengths.

He found that among leaders with this critical mass of competence, 87 percent placed in the top third for annual salary bonuses based on their business performance. More telling, their divisions on average outperformed yearly revenue targets by 15 to 20 percent. Although this study was specific to leaders, it is easy to see how it translates into day-to-day life. People with higher EQs outperform those who have a lower EQ. In fact, scientists could not figure out why people with high IQs outperformed those with average IQs only 20 percent of the time, while people with average IQs outperformed those with high IQs 70 percent of the time in a variety of studies. As it turned out, EQ was the answer.

EQ is so critical that it accounts for 58 percent of performance in all types of jobs. It is the single biggest predictor of performance in the workplace and the strongest driver of leadership and personal excellence.[7]

In a study conducted by Travis Bradberry and Jean Greaves (authors of *Emotional Intelligence 2.0*), they found 90 percent of high performers demonstrate high EQ as opposed to just 20 percent of low performers.

This is not to say that IQ does not account for anything. There are three elements that determine how we think and act: EQ, IQ, and personality. EQ is a flexible skill, whereas IQ and personality are static through life. They do not change.

Your IQ, which is your ability to learn, is the same at age five, fifteen or fifty. We learn more and become smarter; however, our *ability to learn* stays the same. Same with personality, although our beliefs drive our behaviour, when we change our beliefs, our behaviours will change (this is EQ), but our personalities and IQ remain the same.

Think about this for a minute. I will use my daughter as an example. From the moment she was born, she was independent. She full out walked the day she turned seven months old; she negotiated everything from finishing meals to bedtimes to allowance. She never ever slept because she did not want to miss anything, and she was more motherly to her brother—who is only three years her junior—than I was at times. At the time of writing this book, she is twenty years old, and although she has grown so much emotionally, her academic history always remained consistent, which speaks to the fact that her IQ has remained the same: She is still a negotiator—in fact, she is contemplating law school. She is a night owl, rarely going to bed before midnight, and her motherly tendencies have led to her part time job in the daycare, which all speak to the consistency of her personality. The only thing that has changed is her level of emotional intelligence.

All emotions are necessary and serve a purpose. It is how we choose to deal with our emotions that define our behaviours and contribute to who we are as a person.

Fear Smear

Earlier in the book, I shared the story about my friend who bought me Sheryl Sandburg's book *Lean In*. One of the things my friend marked in the book was a comment that Sheryl made:

"Ask yourself; what would I do if I weren't afraid?"[8]

It occurred to me that fear and doubt are the two big barriers that prevent us from following our heart and doing the things we really want to do in life. We have already talked about doubt, so let us take a moment to chat about fear.

I cannot recall the number of times I have been frightened and chose not to do something for fear of what might happen. Oh, what a sheltered life this can be.

When I started my own business, I was terrified. I never aspired to be an entrepreneur. I held a relatively high position in the company I was working for and loved my job. Another firm purchased the company I worked with, and I did not feel that our values were aligned. As you already know, values are important, and if the company you work for has significantly different values than your own, you will never be happy, so I started to explore other options.

At the time, the line of business that I specialized in within the insurance industry had extremely high claim volumes, which meant companies, needed to outsource their claims. This created an opportunity for me to launch an independent adjusting company—so I did. I jumped off that cliff and grew my wings on the way down.

Overcoming fears is like conquering mountains. Now, I'm not saying go out and climb a mountain, unless of course that's what you're into (to each their own), but I am saying pick just one thing you have been procrastinating about or put out of your mind because you were too afraid to do it. It can be something small like asking that cute person to meet you for a coffee or gigantic like quitting your job to pursue your passion or anything in between. It is completely up to you. Now, let's work on figuring out what is triggering the fear and preventing you from acting on this.

Regardless of the reason for fear, it is something that can be overcome with a little effort. In her article "4 Ways to Overcome Your Fears so You Can Achieve Your Dreams"[9] Laura Garnett identifies the number one thing to do is to recognize the trigger that is causing the fear. Once you get to the root cause of the fear, you can tackle and overcome it.

Fear is a physiological experience. It is an emotion we all experience at one time or another. When we feel it, the amygdala (which we already learned about) sends signals to your nervous system. As we know, this has a wide range of effects. Your heart can race, blood pressure goes up, your breathing gets quicker, and adrenaline and cortisol are released.

Now before I go on, it is important to reiterate that every single emotion we experience serves a purpose. There are no "good" or "bad" emotions. They all exist for a reason. The effects of fear served us well in early days when we humans had to protect ourselves in situations where we faced animals that were higher up on the food chain than we were. Fear also serves us in situations where we have to react quickly and rationally to get out of a contentious or dangerous situation; however, for the most part, in modern day, this bodily response to fear can be detrimental.

You have to recognize when this happens and have a strategy to move through it. In order to do this, you will need to identify the trigger. If it is not obvious at first, write down the events surrounding the fear so you can flush out the trigger. Once you have identified the trigger, take a moment to step back and calm your mind. You will need to do whatever works for you here. It may be some deep breathing, a change of scenery, or going for a run or walk. Once you have slowed your mind, get curious about the fear, and ask yourself some questions. You may want to write down your responses. Is the fear rational? What are the best- and worst-case scenarios that will come from doing what it is you fear? What are some things you can do to mitigate the fear? Are negative self-talk or naysayers fuelling your fear? Now that you have identified it, analyzed and rationalized it, it is time to move past it. Think of all the things you have accomplished in life *despite* the fear you may have felt and consider all of the reasons why fear should not prevent you from moving forward.

These steps will help you work through fear regardless of the source. If your fear is centered on failure, you need to know and accept that you will fail, and that failure is a crucial step in success. In his book, *Failing Forward*, John Maxwell discusses embracing failure as a friend and grasping the positive benefits of negative experiences.

When we have a mindset that prepares us for failure and how to learn and grow from these failures, we will be less fearful to venture into the unknown, less reluctant to invest our time and effort into our passion; we will be more willing to "do it afraid". The key is to focus on your strengths, not the things you think you cannot do. When Bob Butera, former president of the New Jersey Devils was asked what makes a winner, his answer was this:

> "What distinguishes winners from losers is that winners concentrate at all times on what they <u>can do</u>, not on what they can't do."

<u>Challenge #14</u>

Describe something you have wanted to do but have not because of fear.

Using the four steps outlined above, work through this fear.

1. Identify the trigger.
2. What will you do to slow down next time the fear is triggered?
3. Ask yourself questions about the fear, get curious.
4. Describe the action you are going to take to move through the fear in order to do what you want to do.

6

Gratitude's the New Attitude

The more you are grateful for what you have, the more you have to be grateful for.

—Zig Ziglar

What's not to be grateful for?

It has been demonstrated time and time again that altruistic people live happier lives. In a study referred to in an *Inc.* magazine article entitled "Gratitude Physically Changes Your Brain"[10], researchers found that practicing gratitude seems to kick off a healthful, self-perpetuating cycle in your brain. It increases willpower and helps keep you calm. The study performed at the Indiana University led by Prathik Kini recruited forty-three subjects suffering from anxiety or depression. Half of the people in the group were asked to write letters of thanks/gratitude to people in their lives. All forty-three underwent brains scans three months later and those that practiced gratitude showed a significant pattern of activity in their brain described as "profound" and "long-lasting" neural effects. Basically, the results suggest that, by identifying what you are thankful for now, it makes it easier to count your blessings later. As a result, the more good you see in your life, the happier and more successful you are likely to be.

I once saw Neil Pasricha, author of *The Book of Awesome* and *The Happiness Equation* deliver a keynote speech at an awards ceremony where I was one of a number of leaders being honoured. At the time, his blog "1000 Awesome Things" was all the rage. He shared with the audience that he started writing this blog as a form of personal therapy. He had recently separated from his wife and lost his best friend to suicide. To keep himself sane, he decided to post one thing a day that to him, was awesome. Most of these were trivial things that we take for granted every day such as hitting a bunch of green lights in a row, bakery air, or when you suddenly remember it is a long weekend. Trivial, but nonetheless quite awesome.

He did a little exercise with the 1000-plus people in the auditorium and asked us to write one thing we thought was awesome and to share it with our neighbour. Imagine the air in the room as everyone reflected on and shared something that made them feel good. Such energy! I remember leaving there that evening thinking wow, such a simple, yet powerful practice. When we really take the time to think about all of the wonderful things in life that make us smile, we can truly appreciate all of the beauty in our world.

The happier you are, the more you recognize and appreciate the value of life and the preciousness of time, and the more you begin to consciously make more of an effort to spend time doing the things you enjoy. This is one vicious cycle that you want to be on!

There are so many things in life to be grateful for, but sometimes it can be hard to articulate every single day. One thing that may help is if you make a gratitude list that you can go back to from time to time. I will share one of mine that I refer to whenever I feel a little down.

> *To be born in a country of freedom and rights*
> *Big fuzzy blankets on cold winter nights*
> *Pinot Noir and a warm bubble bath*
> *The power to choose my own life's path*
> *The support of my friends when I need them the most*
> *My passport that takes me coast to coast*
> *The freedom to run in wide-open spaces*
> *Seeing a double rainbow in small obscure places*
> *Blood moon eclipse in the night's sky*
> *My willingness to give almost anything a try*
> *Curling up in the corner, my own little nook*
> *Cup of tea, my glasses, an inspiring book*

Autumn colours, cool nights, everything fall
Golfing a round without losing a ball
The entrepreneur nature that has grown within
The good sense to recognize and celebrate wins
The failures I've experienced, which I'm now stronger for
The foresight to see beyond a closed door
Sunday morning rain and coffee in bed
Hot yoga and shavasana, time to clear my head
The love and happiness my children bring
Bad karaoke nights, my only chance to sing
Laughing so hard, my cheeks and sides hurt
Spending the day in lulus and a big comfy shirt
Freeing myself from things that no longer serve me
Spending time with my family enjoying Thanksgiving turkey

Of course, you do not have to rhyme it, that's just a quirky thing I like to do!

In John Maxwell's book, *Intentional Living* he says, "It's not what we get that makes us valuable in life. It's what we become in the process that brings value to our lives."[11]

Practicing gratitude can bring great value to our lives while at the same time enriching the lives of others. It truly is a win-win!

> Challenge #15
>
> There are so many ways to practice gratitude. Here are a couple more ideas you can explore.
>
> Keep a positive note box. Write down one good or positive thing that happened that day and put it in a box. Be sure to include who you were with at the time and date it. At end of year, read all the notes.
>
> Keep a gratitude journal and record one to three things you are grateful for each day.
>
> If you keep a traditional journal, end each journal entry with something you are grateful for that has already happened then something you are grateful for that is going to happen in the future (something you desire). For example, I am grateful for the opportunity to work in job that I love and I am grateful for the promotion that I received. (The promotion not actually having happened yet). This plants a seed and wires your brain to start thinking about how to get what you desire.

There's Always More Than Enough

Practicing gratitude also helps us to live with an abundance mindset. Abundance literally means "a very large quantity of something." When we believe there is so much of something to go around, we are not constantly in a competing mindset. Let's take this book, for example. Following my research on the different types of self-help books out there, I found that there were quite a few of them. Some with similar messages, others with a different spin, but so many for readers to choose from. If I lived with a scarcity mindset, I could have convinced myself that there was no point in writing this book because the market was already saturated, but I choose to live with an abundance mindset and believe there are enough readers in the world to go around and enough room in the market for my book too. Plus, of course, my book is awesome! And if I can help just one person live an extraordinary life, even when life may get them down, then that will make it all worthwhile.

Stephen Covey, in his classic *The 7 Habits of Highly Effective People*, explains the concept of abundance and scarcity beautifully:

> *Most people are deeply scripted in what I call the Scarcity Mentality. They see life as having only so much, as though there were only one pie out there. And if someone were to get a big piece of the pie, it would mean less for everybody else.*
>
> *The Scarcity Mentality is the zero-sum paradigm of life. People with a Scarcity Mentality have a very difficult time sharing recognition and credit, power or profit— even with those who help in the production. They also have a hard time being genuinely happy for the success of other people.*
>
> *Abundance Mentality, on the other hand, flows out of a deep inner sense of personal worth or security. It is the paradigm that there is plenty out there and enough to spare for everybody. It results in the sharing of prestige, recognition, profits and decision-making. It opens possibilities, options, alternatives and creativity.*[12]

Covey tells us that when you live in a world of scarcity, you compete for available resources, even when there is an abundance of them.

Living with a prosperity mindset means you are not consumed by what you do not have, you value your unique qualities, capitalize on your strengths and recognize you have what it takes to be all that you want to be, whatever that looks like for you. For some that means success in leading your family in a healthy lifestyle and living in abundance, for others it may be career related and for a few it could be about becoming an entrepreneur. Success, much like beauty is in the eye of the beholder.

Living life with an abundance mindset means you truly believe that there is enough to go around. There is enough money, enough praise at work, enough love, enough friends.

An abundance mindset leads us to want others to succeed in life just as much as we want ourselves to succeed, and this mindset helps us recognize that there is enough awesomeness to go around. We do not have to be successful at the expense of others, nor does the fact that others may have what you want mean there is none (or even less) left for you. An abundance mindset helps us strive to be better every day because each new day is an opportunity to learn, love, live and grow. I have never met a successful person, who lives their life with an attitude of scarcity.

Celebrate Awesomeness

As a society, we need to do a better job of encouraging others to do well. Let's celebrate and embrace awesomeness wherever we find it so in time we will find more of it in ourselves.

I was not always like this. Like many Type A personalities, I felt that people needed to fail in order for me to succeed. Well, maybe that is a little harsh. I did not want people to fail necessarily, but I did want to do better than them. It always felt a little wrong to me, but I knew of no other way. As a woman in business—or any person in business for that matter—it seems you must continually prove yourself, your worth, and your value. "You are only as good as your last win" –and– "What have you done for me lately," were consistent messages when I worked in the corporate environment. How could you possibly consistently prove yourself if you were not better than everyone else was? This is a mindset that can easily be changed, and it all starts with self-leadership.

I have always considered myself a lucky person, not *lottery* lucky, but *life* lucky. Money does not last forever, nor does it bring true happiness. I would rather have things go well for me in life and enjoy life rather than have millions of dollars and be miserable. I did not realize, until I read John Maxwell's *21 Irrefutable Laws of Leadership*, that the luck I experienced was really more about the law of intuition rather than pure magical leprechaun luck. This law suggests who you are dictates what you see. It is founded on the premise that everybody is intuitive in his or her area of strength. Although I would not have always said this, I can confidently now say that one of my areas of strength is leadership. I still have a lot of growing to do in this regard, and so I continue to study, read, learn, and apply new things every single day. I have done a lot of work on my emotional intelligence (which we previously spent some time discussing) and myself. That work has truly allowed me to see life through a completely new lens.

In studying the law of intuition, I learned almost every time a person is in the right place at the right time, other people are in the same place at the same time too—the leader is just more aware. After learning this, I had something of an epiphany and realized, *yes, I have done things at the right time or been in the right place at the right time, but much of the success that came out of those times was as a result of my ability to read trends and anticipate needs.* They say success happens when preparedness meets opportunity. When we are constantly preparing for our heart's desire, then we are ready for the opportunities as they present themselves.

Now I say this with the caveat that things will not always go your way. In fact, I have experienced my fair share of downs, detours, and bumps in the road. Although I have struggled through some difficult times, I embraced each and every one of them with an eye towards learning the lessons they were meant to bring. Things will not always be perfect in life, and yes, sometimes life will suck, but if you are able to reflect on the awesomeness that lives within, you will still feel content during tumultuous times.

To be awesome we must be leaders. Not leaders in the traditional sense (although you may very well be that too) but leaders of life. We must be able to lead ourselves, and as a natural by-product of this, others may want to follow. What you choose to do with your leadership abilities outside of making yourself and your life awesome is a personal decision and one only you can make. However, one thing is for certain, the more we celebrate the awesomeness in others, the more of it we will find in ourselves.

My friend and colleague Kadey Shultz is truly amazing at this. They say less than 3 percent of the world's leaders are "natural born" leaders, well Kadey is one of them! She has such charisma and charm. She is one of those women who lights up a room the minute she sets foot through the door. She constantly celebrates others—women especially—and brings out the best in people by acknowledging every accomplishment and achievement no matter how trivial or insignificant they themselves may believe it to be. Being on the receiving end of Kadey's encouragement, I have witnessed this first hand.

After spending several years working as a lawyer in the insurance industry, Kadey ventured out into the unknown in 2015 and launched a new firm with her partner, Jason Frost. Kadey is an accomplished litigator and has won several awards including Top Lawyers under 40 (2015), Lexpert US/Canada Litigators to Watch (2014) and Canadian Defence Lawyers Exceptional Young Lawyer Award just to name a few! However, it is not these awards that define Kadey. Of course, they are extremely prestigious, well deserved, and speak volumes to her expertise, passion, and drive, but what I love about Kadey goes deeper than that. Kadey is one of the few people I know who is genuinely passionate about inspiring and celebrating others. She does a lot of volunteering within the industry and sits on the board of directors of Holland Bloorview Kids Rehab Hospital Foundation, working to raise funds for the Biggar Endowment to end Duchenne Muscular Dystrophy. She was inspired to contribute by her son, Emery, as he battles this horrific disease.

As a mother of two, wife, entrepreneur, litigator, educator, speaker, volunteer, and lifter of women everywhere, I knew Kadey would be a perfect contributor to this book, and in true Kadey fashion, she was happy to help. When asked how Kadey manages to be her best self every day, she shared that knowing her core values is what is important to her and is what has driven how she has developed her career, family, and not-for-profit life.

She goes on to say that, she is of a generation that was raised to be pleasers, and this can create barriers to alignment. Instead of focusing on how you tick and what makes you tick, these things are put on the back burner because you are wired to want to please others. If you are working on pleasing someone else, then you need to refocus. Really knowing your values helps you with this. Your values should not alter too much over the years. How you express them may change; however, fundamentally, they remain the same.

Even on a really hard day, these core values guide Kadey. She also shares that it is important not to identify yourself in the moment as being positive or negative, a success or a failure. Her values are not about defining herself based on one beat. It is about consistency and longevity. We live in such an instantaneous world. We are constantly exposed to immediate gratification or criticism. We need to be sure to look at our cumulative efforts and sustained behaviours, which she jokes, can sometimes be difficult for her based on her own behaviours. Nonetheless, it is important to view things through this lens of consistency.

Kadey acknowledges that life can be difficult at times. She is a business owner and a mother and has a son with health challenges—there are many pressures. We all have bad days. Kadey does not allow that bad day to control the beat of her life.

Lastly, Kadey shares that being her best self involves being comfortable with discomfort. Doing this is a skillset. It is not about *not* experiencing the feeling of discomfort at all. It is about identifying with it, understanding the nature of the discomfort, and working through it. Often for Kadey, discomfort will arise if she is in a new space, outside the realm of her known world. She reminds herself that it is okay to be uncomfortable because this is a place of growth and that focusing on the growth spectrum will help her through the discomfort. Many of us have experienced the belief that we have to be over prepared or perfect, but this is not true. When faced with these feelings, Kadey reminds herself that she does not have to be perfect and embraces the discomfort knowing she will have grown because of it.

Kadey's story goes to support so many of the principles in this book and emulates what many others have shared. She is truly an extraordinary woman, and I am grateful to her for sharing her insight with me so I could in turn could share with you in the hopes that it will inspire you to find the awesomeness in you and in others.

In 2013, I assumed the president's role of the Ontario Insurance Adjuster's Association. It is tradition for the first edition of the *WP* magazine (it stands for *Without Prejudice*) to do an expose on the incoming president. A writer is hired to interview the incoming president as well as their friends and family members with the view of giving the members of the association a glimpse of their new president. As I was preparing for the interview, my mother introduced me to this poem because, in her words, it reminded her of me. As I read it, it reminded me of so many great people that I have been fortunate enough to know in my life and I think it touches on some of the things we have discussed here so it seems fitting for me to share it with all of you. It's called "Wide Open," from *I Will Not Die An Unlived Life: Finding Purpose and Passion* by Dawna Markova, PhD.

Wide Open

I will not die an unlived life
I will not live in fear
of falling or catching fire.
I choose to inhabit my days,
to allow my living to open me,
to make me less afraid,
more accessible,
to loosen my heart
until it becomes a wing,
a torch, a promise.
I choose to risk my significance;
to live so that which came to me as seed
goes to the next as blossom
and that which came to me as blossom,
goes on as fruit.

dawnamarkova@ptpinc.org

How beautiful a world it would be if we all celebrated and elevated ourselves and others.

Challenge #16

Describe a time when you were envious of someone else for something they had acquired or something they accomplished. How did it make you feel?

Take this same situation and write a short note congratulating the person on their recent accomplishment or acquisition (if you send it to them, even better!). Now, think about how this made you feel.

Make a difference

Have you ever done something for someone who could never pay you back? Have you made an anonymous donation or a kind gesture that no-one will ever know of? We already know from the beginning of this chapter that practicing gratitude can have a significant positive impact on our life, and furthermore, according to a 2013 study, doing good has a substantial impact on our lives as well!

Doing good decreases stress, increases life expectancy, and makes us feel better. Some of the results of various studies are astounding. Findings show that subjects who provided tangible assistance to friends or family members (running errands, helping with childcare, etc.), reported less stressful events and, consequently, had reduced mortality. In other words, "helping others reduced mortality specifically by buffering the association between stress and mortality."[13]

In a 2010 study, it was found that the less people gave money away, the higher their cortisol levels, which is your body's main stress hormone. When we do good, our brain releases endorphins (the happy chemical), so doing good literally makes us feel better. Not only that, after an extensive review of forty studies on the effect of volunteering on general health and happiness, the BMC Public Health journal has concluded that volunteering is also good for mental health.[14] The review found that, along with improved well-being and life satisfaction, volunteering is also linked to decreased depression.

I will never forget one time I was preparing a speech for an annual charity auction and dinner. I happen to be on a call with one of my mentors and mentioned that I have such a difficult time asking people to donate money.

"Tammie," he said, "why are you being so selfish?"

"I think you are missing the point," I said. "I am *trying* help. I am just struggling with the ask."

And then he said it again.

"Why are you being so selfish? How does it make you feel to know that what you do has a direct impact on the lives of others?"

"It is one of the most rewarding feelings in the world," I said.

"Well then," he said, "why would you keep that feeling all to yourself? Why would you not want to give others the opportunity to give money and have an impact on the lives of others and experience this feeling for themselves? Think about the change that has taken place within you and how much your life has been enriched. You are not *asking* them for anything. You are giving them *opportunity* to gain in so many ways both spiritually and emotionally."

It was one of those a-ha moments for me because he was right. Earning money may contribute to your success, but giving money contributes to a life of significance, and who doesn't want a life of significance? Clearly, I needed to stop being so selfish!

So now is the perfect time to share a little more with you about the charity I mentioned, especially since some of the proceeds from every book sold will be going to support it.

One of my favourite things about people is learning about their story. We all have one. Sometimes it is a love story, other times a comedy, a little drama may show up here and there but often times it can be a heartbreaking story. One of the most gratifying things we can do as human beings is to help others during the heartbreaking chapters of their lives.

When I started my business in 2008, there were many things I was unsure of, but one thing I did know for certain was that I have been truly blessed in my life. I firmly believe that we, as a society, should give back whenever and however we can, whether it is volunteering in the community, paying it forward, or donating money to support a charity or cause. So I recruited my two children, then eleven and eight, and we went to work right away to find a corporate charity that we would call our own.

After much research—surfing websites, reading print material and watching DVDs (YouTube wasn't really a big charity thing back then)—we chose the Jennifer Ashleigh Children's Charity (JACC), which we were not familiar with at the time. We recognized that JACC was different for a number of reasons, but what we really loved about them was the fact that they seemed to fill a gap and take care of families that would otherwise fall through the cracks by providing direct financial assistance to families with seriously ill children. We knew that, as much as these children needed things, wishes, and items to make their lives more comfortable, their illness inevitably brings along serious financial strain. One or both parents may need to leave their jobs to care for their child, resulting in much needed medication, treatment, or even the necessities of life becoming out of financial reach for them. By financially assisting, JACC is helping to facilitate a new "normal" life for these wonderful families.

Working closely over the years with the phenomenal people associated with JACC only went to further validate that this is truly a remarkable charity. From the Founder, Norm himself, to the families that we help, gratefulness and gratitude never go unnoticed. It gave us great pleasure to be able to corporately sponsor and fundraise for JACC over the eight years I owned the business, and now I am immensely grateful for the opportunity to serve as the President of the Board of Directors.

Now to share the story of the remarkable man behind the charity, a great mentor, a selfless philanthropist with the purest of hearts, and an inspiration to so many, Norman Clements. I could not even begin to give justice to Norm in my own words, so I am happy to share an excerpt of Norm's biography written by his niece Corina.

> *There are those who allow tough circumstances to sour and harden them. Others face those difficult times and grow into better people. When Alice Clements was unexpectedly left a young widow, alone to raise her five kids—ranging from 9 months old to Norm at 17 years old—she chose to do everything possible to keep her family together. This environment of sticking together through the tough times and hard work coupled with a deep faith in God shaped Norman's character and life.*
>
> *After his father's death, Norman shouldered the responsibility of sorting through and closing down his dad's business. As the oldest sibling, he did not shy away from working long hours to help support his family.*

Delivering papers to downtown newspaper boxes from 1 AM to 7 AM made it difficult to stay awake in school, yet he never complained or gave up. He held a number of jobs over the years, which included working for a moving company, selling "Fuller brushes" and growing and selling Christmas trees.

Norm was never one to sit around and wait for an opportunity to materialize, he made them happen! When he was young, he started driving from school to school selling gym clothing out of the trunk of his old car. This venture grew into 37 years of retail stores operating across southern Ontario. Being "owner" and "president" of a successful business as well as co-owner of the "greatest pacer in Harness racing" never went to Norm's head. He could still be seen helping on cash at a 60-hour sale, or heard saying something kind about the driver or trainer. Norm was never one to take the glory for himself.

Norman and his siblings inherited their mother's desire to help others. The burden she carried did not deter her from reaching out to others. Norman's mother looked after other small children on a regular basis, and at church, she was the first to invite visiting missionaries home for lunch. She could not go to another country to serve but was committed to supporting and praying for them. Three of her children became missionaries to foreign countries while Norman and his youngest brother dedicated themselves to business to wholeheartedly support their siblings.

Norm's soft heart for others, especially the underdog, took root during his childhood and has never faded. A common sight in his home has always been extra plates at the table or someone sleeping on the couch. Norman was always willing to give a dropout a job, a recovering alcoholic a helping hand and a needy single mom help with her rent. He would buy a van full of fresh vegetables to encourage someone at the flea market and think nothing of the three-hour round trip to deliver it to a drop-in centre for homeless youth in downtown Toronto. He wouldn't just drop off fresh pastries or fruit at some lonely seniors' homes, he'd take the time to drink a cup of tea, try one of their cabbage rolls or listen to some memory they wanted to share, and this is someone always busy in some business project, yet never too busy for someone in need.

When his baby granddaughter, born on his birthday, died from Spinal Muscular Atrophy, it spurred Norm on to start the "Jennifer Ashleigh Children's Charity". Since 1990 they have helped thousands of families who needed a hand through tough times dealing with seriously ill children with simple necessities (yet often overlooked) like providing transportation to a medical appointment, a few hours of respite care or money to buy fresh fruits or vegetables to assist in a healthy diet for a child who has undergone chemotherapy. This charity is a reflection of Norm's heart. It is not about big flashy donations, it is all about lightening a burden, being a safety net and helping to keep someone going especially through tough times. For Norm and his charity, these families have names, faces, stories and dreams.

I have been privileged to see these qualities in Norman because he is my uncle, but also, I have been able to develop a closer relationship with him because one day

22 years ago he came alongside of me and asked what my dreams were. He helped that dream come true by sharing his time, money, and heart to support a training program for kids getting off the streets in Bolivia.

After more than 20 years of coming to Bolivia, Norman can still only say about 10 words in Spanish and even then with a strong accent, but his joy and love spans the language barrier. He will always have half a dozen people happily peeling the potatoes or cutting the onions for the countless meals he prepares for children's homes, rehabilitation centres, street kids, jail, volunteers, and the lonely security guard down the street.

Others might use their holidays to lie on the beach or enjoy a cruise, but Norman spends 3 weeks every year sweating buckets in the 40 degree, humid kitchen, cooking and carving 120+ roasts to freeze for our "Christmas on the Streets" meal. Some might think that "street kids" do not need the best cut of meat, but Norman does not skimp when it comes to giving, even when it is for kids who maybe have never seen more meat than soup bones and chicken feet.

Giving and helping are not something Norman does, it is who he is. He shares much more than his pocketbook; he shares his heart and life. The greatest gift that Uncle Norman gives so freely to others is himself.

Truly an inspiration. Norm is a man of values, integrity, and resilience. One day before a board meeting, Norm and I sat so I could interview him for this book. His words and stories were fascinating; I became so entrenched in what he was saying that often times I would forget to take the notes!

As we know from the beautifully written bio shared by Corina, in addition to a philanthropist, Norm was a businessman. He had a lot of successful times during his business career, but Norm also experienced horrible times as his company faced bankruptcy with over 800 people relying on him to provide them and their families with a livelihood, Norm was devastated. This took a significant toll on his mental well-being, and he could not get out of bed for days. He worked through this funk with daily devotions (words from scripture) and inspirational messages. He shared that when one of these messages would hit him in the heart, it would give him the motivation to move forward. Norm jokes, the only time you become a loser is when you refuse to get up. You have little control over many things in life, but you always have control over how to deal with them (as discussed in the Power of Choice chapter). Norm used to be a bit of a vindictive thinker, if someone hurt him, he'd think about what he could do to get them back, but he realized this was not the way to live life. Now, if someone does something bad to Norm, he retaliates by doing something heartwarming to him or her in return.

True friends are also important in life, Norm explains. When he was going through his difficult time, he had a couple of very wealthy friends, neither of whom ever offered to lend a helping hand in any way, shape or form. The help came from a man Norm had met just once in passing. Obviously, a man with a true pure heart. His point being, to be your best you, be a person who offers encouragement to others. Encouragement can be anything, a cup of coffee, a kind word or doing a favour for someone without them ever knowing you did it.

Norm says he goes to Bolivia for the sole purpose of helping his niece Corina. He says he does this for selfish reasons because he gets so much joy out of others being happy. To see the smiles on the faces of the families and children while Norm is there helping in the community is his motivation to go back year after year. The same goes for the JACC Country BBQ, which is held at his farm in Uxbridge, Ontario, each year. This is a day where JACC families, donors, and volunteers come together to celebrate JACC kids. The property is set up with so many activities for the kids to enjoy such as face painting, fishing, petting zoos, dancing and more. There is food, fun, music and smiles all day long. Norm spends his day transporting the families in the JACC trolley bus from the top of the property—where everyone parks down—to the bottom where all the festivities are. Why does he do this? Because he loves to see the smiles on all the kids faces as they get on board the trolley in anticipation of all the fun they are about to have. I must admit, I look forward to this event every year for exactly the same reason!

Norm describes his mother as his mentor and best friend. If he ever walked into the house with a big head (inflated ego), she would shrink it, and when he was hurting, she would inflate him. Her words of wisdom to Norm included things such as "take one day at a time" –and– "do one nice thing a day" –and– "be responsible for what you do, not what other people do."

When asked what Norm does to be his best self, he says he always tries to look for the good in someone and find something nice to say to them. He chooses his words wisely, and if they are spiteful or going to hurt someone's feelings, he bites his tongue. Picking and choosing his battles is another tactic Norm uses. Sometimes, you just have to let things slide and having a good attitude goes a long way. Norm always tries to set the example. He will clean the toilet himself before asking someone else to do it.

When things get a little rough during hard times, Norm takes a walk, a drive, or does what he needs to so he can clear his head. He says that sometimes we get into a box and do not know how to get out of it. We need to create the space in our heads to allow us to find the clarity we need to move forward.

Norm is truly a remarkable man. I am so grateful to be even just a little part of Norm's life through the Jennifer Ashleigh Children's Charity.

Challenge #17

Describe a time someone did something for you that truly made a difference in your life. How did that person help, and what impact did it have on your life?

Think of a time when you went out of your way to help another person. Describe how that made you feel.

Describe one thing you can do for someone else that will better their lives.

7

Be Devilishly Selfish While Loving Others

It is good to have an end to journey toward, but it's the journey that matters in the end.

—Ernest Hemingway

At the Core

One of my best friends, Steven DelGreco, is a person whom I admire dearly. Anyone who knows Steve will most definitely question why I have reserved his story for this chapter in the book about being "selfish" because he is probably the least selfish person I know. He is genuine, kind, caring, and loves almost everyone, and most everyone loves him. He is a person of great value who adds value to others' lives daily. At any given time, there is someone calling on Steve for his insight, wisdom, or advice. He and his wife Donna, with whom I am equally as close, do very well for themselves yet live relatively simple lives in the city with their dog Barney. They enjoy the important things in life like family, travel, good friends, and great wine.

Steve was the first person I spoke to about contributing to this book. He consistently shows up in life whether as a husband, friend, colleague, mentor, or student. Steve is Steve regardless of the day or circumstance and spends most of his days being the best version of himself he can be. When I asked Steve to share his secret with me, he said there is a fine line between being selfish and being true to yourself. Wow. Sheer brilliance!

To be true to yourself, you must live by your values. There are no right or wrong values, they are personal and intrinsically tied to who you are as a person. Steve explains that being true to himself and his values gets him through every decision and obstacle in life. He credits his parents for instilling such strong values in him at a very early age and while instilling these values, they encouraged him to be his own person, to do what was right for him. Being armed with strong moral values gave him the strength and confidence, which allowed him to believe in himself, refrain from peer pressure and being sucked into negativity.

Steve jokes that being true to yourself does not mean there is a pot of gold at the end of the rainbow. He tries to see things from other people's perspectives, which I would have to say is one of Steve's greatest strengths. He tries to be a good person and make a positive difference in the lives of others, and although he says you may not always get rewarded for doing the right thing, when living by your values, you can be confident that you will face challenges with strong conviction and know that whatever decision you make will be in line with your morals.

When Steve is working through a problem—or if he is stuck—he reflects on his values and what he believes in, assesses the end game in order to seek clarity on how to get there, and relies on the people closest to him for strength, support, and validation.

Having strong values has a direct impact on your beliefs and, therefore, your mindset. What we believe about our values dictates how we show up in life. Steve goes on to say humans are very good at fooling themselves so, when you ask questions of yourself, you must answer them honestly. If you do not, you are only fooling yourself. If you do not like the answers you are hearing or seeing, it may be time to revisit those values.

Steve shared this poem with me, which really demonstrates how he lives, and I am excited to share it with you. It was written by Dale Wimbrow and published in 1934 in *The American* magazine.

> *The Guy in the Glass*
>
> *When you get what you want in your struggle for pelf,*
> *And the world makes you King for a day,*
> *Then go to the mirror and look at yourself,*

And see what that guy has to say.

For it isn't your Father, Mother or Wife,
Who judgement upon you must pass,
The feller whose verdict counts most in your life,
Is the guy staring back from the glass.

He's the feller to please, never mind all the rest,
For he's with you clear to the end,
And you've passed your most dangerous, difficult test,
If the guy in the glass is your friend.

You may be like Jack Horner and "chisel" a plum,
And think you're a wonderful guy,
But the man in the glass says you're only a bum
If you can't look him straight in the eye.

You can fool the whole world down the pathway of years,
And get pats on the back as you pass,
But the final reward will be heartache and tears,
If you've cheated the guy in the glass.

We only have ourselves to be accountable to, so this is what I mean when I say, be devilishly selfish. Your values are yours, and mine are mine, nobody else's. We can't steal them, lend them out or break up with them. Remaining true to our values allows us to be comfortable with our decisions and choices and dictates how we show up in life for ourselves and others.

> ### Challenge #18
>
> Ask yourself the following questions and record your answers.
>
> What are the values that guide you, and are these values serving you?
>
> On your deathbed, when you assess who you were, what do you foresee? What do you want to see?
>
> Looking back on your life, what do you want others to say about the type of person you were on earth?

Remember Steve's words of wisdom when answering these questions. When you ask questions of yourself, you must answer them honestly. If you do not you are only fooling yourself.

Success Is Not Final – Failure Is Not Fatal

As previously discussed, shortly after another firm acquired the company I was working for, I decided to start my own insurance adjusting business. At the time, I had been in the industry for approximately thirteen years and worked in a niche field handling injury claims. I worked as a consultant for about six months while I developed my business plan, strategized, and went to market. My three-year plan went something like this: handle files on my own and work from home for the first year and then moderate growth with the addition of two people and an office in year two, progressing to five people and generating revenues of approximately $800,000 in year three.

As I approached key clients in the first six months, it became evident that there was much more of a need for this type of service than I had anticipated. I was being asked to take on hundreds of files in short periods. I hired immediately to accommodate the requests and moved into an executive centre office space with a core group of about six people by the end of year one.

A friend of mine whom I previously worked with had bought me a money tree to celebrate the business and opening of our new office. Now, you have to understand, I had never been good with plants. Anything green in my house is either located in the fridge by way of a jar of pickles or in the form of one of those fake plants or trees. But this was a money tree! I was determined to nurture it, love it, and see it flourish. It was symbolic to me, and it is important to this story for reasons you will later understand.

Business continued to grow beyond my expectations to the point that, at our peak, just a short two and a half years after launching, we were a $4 million company with thirty-two employees. The money tree was flourishing!

Shortly prior to hitting our peak, the government announced some legislative changes that were going to drastically affect the viability of our business. You see, the claims that we specialized in were going to be significantly reduced based on these new policy changes, which meant the insurance companies would no longer need to outsource. I was going to have to rethink our strategy and look at diversifying to keep the business alive. We saw a steady decline in revenue from $4 million in 2010 to $3.5 million in 2011 and less than a million in 2013. As the revenues reduced, so did the staff. As people resigned to take work in a more stable insurer environment, they would be in tears because they did not want to leave the team we had built together. We had truly become a family.

I have a very strong internal sense of control. I am a firm believer that we are makers of our own destiny, that everything happens for a reason, and that positive thinking leads to positive results. With that in mind, I tried a number of things to turn the business around. I conducted market research, developed some new offerings, and continued to invest money into the business as we continued to lose money month over month and year over year. I was tied to some expensive leases that I could not get out of and was assessed with a significant tax debt. At the same time, the money tree was dying. It became infested with bugs and lost its beautiful green lustre. I became consumed with keeping this plant alive somehow, believing that the success of the business was contingent upon the health of the money tree, but nothing worked. The business was still struggling, and the plant was still dying.

Although we experienced some great success in the seven plus years I owned the business, I made many mistakes as well. I had ridden the entrepreneur roller coaster of life from the financial struggles associated with starting a business with my own capital to success and back down to failure. I learned many lessons. However, I would have to say the lesson of the money tree is what resonates most. I spent a great deal of time, effort, and energy trying to bring that tree (and by association the business) back to life. It was not until I realized it was okay to let go and physically took the tree to the trash—emotionally accepting the fact that success is not final, and failure is not fatal—that I could truly move forward and venture on to the next chapter of my life.

In John Maxwell's book *Failing Forward*, he tells us that all roads to achievement lead through the land of failure. If we have not failed, we have not learned. Just because we have failed at something does not make us a failure. Maxwell shares seven abilities[15] of achievers that enable them to fail, not take it personally, and keep moving forward:

Reject Rejection
See failure as temporary
See failures as isolated incidents
Keep realistic expectations
Focus on strengths
Vary approach to achievement
Bounce back

I think number seven is the most important. We must have the strength and willingness to bounce back. By acknowledging steps one through six and taking some time to reflect and learn from our failures, we bounce back stronger and wiser than before.

Reflection is something I had never really practiced until a few years ago, and I continue to work on my consistency with it. For a period of a couple of years I was religious with my journaling; now it's less frequent, but I do take the opportunity to reflect almost daily whether it's a few minutes in the morning, before heading into a meeting, or before bed. Reflection is important for a number of reasons. It helps us learn more about ourselves, process emotions, appreciate the good in our lives and strategize on how to change the things that are not so good in our lives. If nothing else, it provides us with a space to be selfish. To not worry about others or expend energy on anyone else. It gives us time with ourselves whether it be minutes, hours, or days.

It benefits us on all three planes—physically, mentally, and spiritually.

The level of reflection is irrelevant, it can be as light as you want or as deep as you need. I have practiced levels of reflection ranging from one extreme to the other—from taking a full weekend retreat to reflect on life and my goals to very light reflections that consist of a minute or two following a conversation with someone. Reflection can be intense, mellow, or fun.

Earlier I mentioned that I had gone to Paraguay on a leadership training initiative. What I haven't shared with you yet is my journey getting there. From Toronto, it was a three-flight adventure. My itinerary was Toronto to Punta Cana, Punta Cana to Panama, then Panama to Asunción (the capital of Paraguay). The first flight to Punta Cana was uneventful. When I arrived in Panama, I headed to the Copa lounge for some food and a drink. I thought my flight out of Panama to Paraguay left at 11:15 PM that evening. I headed down to the gate around 9:30 PM to see if I could find any of my John Maxwell Team (JMT) colleagues. There were many people in this gate area that serviced three different flights. I saw a flight to Paraguay on the board and assumed this was mine. As some time passed, I looked again and the flight on the board was gone. It was now around 11:00 PM, and I was starting to panic. I managed to find an attendant that spoke a little bit of English and he tried to explain that my flight had left much earlier in the evening. In fact, it left at 9:15 PM, not 11:15 PM. I managed to miss the flight altogether and there was not another leaving for Paraguay until the morning. By the time I sorted this all with the desk, it was after midnight, and I had to be at the Copa airline counter at 6:00 AM to try to get myself on the next flight out. There was no point in going to a hotel now, so I slept in the airport.

I am not sure if you have ever been stranded in the airport of a Third World country, but it is certainly no Ritz Carleton—or even a Motel 6 for that matter. There were a few bench style chairs with arms that did not lift so there was no lying down, and it was eerily deserted. I did the best I could in the environment I was in and made it through the night. At 6:00 AM, I was the second person in line at the Copa counter waiting for them to open. As it turned out, they could not get me on a flight before 9:15 PM that evening, so guess what, I had to spend a whole new day in the Panama Airport. I could either laugh or cry. Well, actually, I did spend some time crying, but then I spent some time writing and reflecting. I kept this reflection super light and comical; otherwise, I probably would have been ready to hop on the next flight home. I still look at it from time to time to remind me of this opportunity of a lifetime because being stranded in Panama was a part of the whole experience and what a phenomenal overall experience it was. I call this one "Tales from the Kip"

Top 10 things I have learned after being stranded at an airport for over 24 hours...

1. *I need to brush up on my Spanish*
2. *I cannot sleep sitting up no matter how tired I am*
3. *Copa lounge has two shift changes throughout the day, and they have good wine*
4. *I like the taco salad at Margaritaville, the coconut shrimp, not so much*
5. *My butt is not meant to be sat on for this long*
6. *It takes me three times as long to write an article when tired*
7. *My eyes are swollen, but I can still see*

8. I am super sensitive to the sound of children's screams or to anyone's sounds for that matter
9. There are three Lacoste stores in this airport for some strange reason
10. You can get a free plane ticket if you cry long enough (did I mention that Copa Airlines felt so bad for me, they did not charge me for my new ticket?)

Although this next part really has nothing to do with reflection, I feel compelled to share it with you because this is how I met the beautiful Louise Elliott whose story I shared with you earlier.

As it turned out, there were a number of other JMTers who were stranded in Panama due to delayed flights and missed connections. The difference was they were in hotels, for the most part, because their missed flights were due to airline delays and not stupidity (like mine). JMT coaches have a private Facebook group, and there were a number of us posting to the group page as we travelled from all over the world to come together. Louise, who I did not know at the time, posted to the page that she was stranded in Panama. I responded to her to let her know that I was also stranded and suggested we meet for lunch at Margaritaville (which was the only restaurant in the airport). We met and immediately hit it off. We had such a great time together in Paraguay and continued to maintain a relationship even though she lives in Ohio and I in Toronto. So you see, it wasn't all for naught. Had I not been stranded in the airport, Louise and I would never have developed the bond we did, and I would not be sitting here telling you about her today.

> Challenge #19
>
> Describe a situation you experienced this week (good or not so good).
>
> Take two to five minutes to think about the situation from beginning to end and describe:
>
> 1. What evoked the situation
> 2. How it made you feel (what emotion was aroused)
> 3. Was the emotion appropriate for the situation
> 4. How you handled the situation and your emotion
> 5. What you would do differently next time
>
> Congratulations, you have just reflected!

Forgiveness is the next best medicine

We must learn not only to forgive others but also to forgive ourselves. Sometimes that is even harder to do.

During a hot yoga session one morning, the instructor shared with us that she had been practicing the philosophy of Ho'oponopono. As she described the foundation of this philosophy, it warmed my heart. I immediately came home and researched this beautiful practice. Ho'oponopono is an ancient Hawaiian practice of reconciliation and forgiveness. It has evolved over the years and was modernized by Dr. Ihaleakala Hew Len, who has cured an entire ward of criminally insane patients without ever even meeting them. I encourage you to read his story.

The practice, which is still widely used today, is based on the premise that you can heal others by healing yourself and consists of four steps; repentance, forgiveness, gratitude, and love. Whether forgiving yourself or someone else, the mantra of the Ho'oponopono remains the same;

I'm sorry
I forgive you
Thank you and
I love you

Nothing more than these words needs to be said although, feel free to add context.

Forgiving yourself may sound something like this:

I'm sorry I doubted myself
Please forgive me for succumbing to those thoughts
Thank you for being judgement free
I love you, you are always enough

Alternatively, if forgiving someone else:

I am sorry you felt the need to raise your voice with me
Please forgive me for not understanding your frame of mind
Thank you for sharing your frustration with me
I love you for all that you are

The practice of Ho'oponopono is about healing yourself by taking absolute responsibility for your life. Through this practice, Dr. Len discovered that loving yourself is the greatest way to improve yourself, and as you improve yourself, you improve your world.

For those who may not feel comfortable with the language of this forgiveness practice, you may be more receptive to William Fergus Martin's *Four steps to forgiveness*[16]. It is a similar approach using different terminology. The four steps in his process are as follows:

> Step 1: State who you need to forgive and for what.
>
> Step 2: Honestly acknowledge how you currently feel about the situation.
>
> Step 3: State the benefits you will get from forgiving. This will mainly be the opposite of what you are currently feeling. Sadness will become happiness, anger will become peace, heaviness becomes a feeling of lightness and so on. If you are not sure about the benefits just choose a few general good feelings which you would like to have for now (happier, more at ease, more confident etc.).
>
> Step 4: Commit yourself to forgiving. This is simply stating who you intend to forgive and then acknowledging the benefits, which come from forgiving.

Regardless of the method or approach you choose to use for forgiveness, the important thing is that you forgive. Anger, hostility, grudges, and revenge will never serve you or allow you to live an extraordinary life while being your best you.

> <u>Challenge #20</u>
>
> I am pretty sure you know where I am going with this one! Take a moment to identify someone you need to forgive (it could be yourself) and work through each of the four steps using whichever process resonates with you.

Know you are always enough

I have had the same hairdresser since I was eighteen years old. I always joke about the fact he is the longest male relationship I have had in my life excluding my immediate family. Chris is the owner of VIP Hairways in Markham, Ontario. He is a very successful entrepreneur. He has built a wonderfully successful business, developed numerous products, and trained hundreds of professionals over the years, and above all, he is the most straightforward person I have ever met. You always know what you are going to get when you are with Chris, no matter who is in his chair or in the shop at the time, Chris will always tell you what is on his mind. He calls a spade a spade, will challenge you if you happen to be down on yourself, and will always find a way to make you see the truth. He speaks in analogies and tells the best stories. Chris is an incredible example of a man who lives life to the fullest while being true to himself each day.

When I asked him to share one thing that helps him be the best version of himself he can be, he of course, shared two. First, he said that he wakes up every day with the view of helping another person become better than who they are. All of us, regardless of our personalities or who we are, can benefit from others and appreciate the differences in people. We need to use those differences to impact the lives of others. The second thing he mentioned was that he never makes a decision based on self-degradation. He shares that we as a society tend to be self-degrading. We are so hard on ourselves and others, and when we make decisions through this lens, it brings the evil out in all of us. We must practice humanity towards ourselves and others and when we do that, we bring out the light in everyone. The best way to do this is to love ourselves for who we are, and then the love for others will follow. So true.

This brings me to my friend Nicki. I met Nicki Scott at a leadership conference in San Diego. Nicki is one of those people who makes you feel immediately at ease the minute you meet her. She has such a soft and caring disposition and a genuine curiosity of others. She is full of passion, vigour and vitality and is always looking for ways to help people in their journey of life. She has spent eighteen years as a Rotarian, travelling the world, developing their leaders, and speaking at international conventions and district conferences.

As I came to know Nicki, I admired all of the things she was doing and her attitude towards life despite having gone through some very difficult times. We kept in touch, and by the time I had started to write my book, Nicki had moved to Cotswolds, England. I reached out to her to set up a call in hopes of her agreeing to contribute to the book. Little did I know, at the exact time I reached out to her, she happened to be in Toronto for a Rotary Convention. It was pure serendipity! This meeting was clearly destined to be! We met for dinner the following night. We reminisced and had some laughs, and Nicki shared some beautiful insights with me about her journey in the quest to find her purpose in life.

She started down this road in 2008, following a conversation with her aunt who mentioned that she was worried about her. She felt that Nicki was so busy chasing "success" that she was missing life. This was an a-ha moment for Nicki, she was determined to take a step back and really think about the life she wanted to live and what success meant to her. She did some work with Eckhart Tolle and *Creating a New Earth* which is all about finding your purpose in life. She did a lot of introspection during this time. One of the key insights that came out of this journey for Nicki was to know that you are always enough. We must allow ourselves to have less than perfect days and, even on those days, still know that we are enough. We should never lose sight of this. She shared this Marianne Williamson quote with me. It is from her book *A Return to Love*.

> *Our deepest fear is not that we are inadequate. Our deepest fear is that we are powerful beyond measure. It is our light, not our darkness that most frightens us. We ask ourselves, Who am I to be brilliant, gorgeous, talented, fabulous? Actually, who are you* not *to be? You are a child of God. Your playing small does not serve the world. There is nothing enlightened about shrinking so that other people won't feel insecure around you. We are all meant to shine, as children do. We were born to make manifest the glory of God that is within us. It's not just in some of us; it's in everyone. And as we let our own light shine, we unconsciously give other people permission to do the same. As we are liberated from our own fear, our presence automatically liberates others.*[17]

Nicki made the choice to let her light shine. She shares that if you are constantly trying to control your life, you are going to be missing it. The universe is meant to work with us. If we let go of control and work with the universe, life will flow to us, for us and through us! Everything we go through in life has to flow. Nicki says that when she got out of her own way and stayed rooted in purpose as opposed to success, her life began to flow much more serendipitously. She jokes that she does not have all the answers, but she knows that her higher self certainly does, and we need to give ourselves the space to find those answers within us. We all have the capacity to be who we want to be, and we must forge ahead on our own path, not the path everyone else thinks we should be on.

Nicki shares that being your best you is not synonymous with being perfect. There is no perfection in the world, nor should you try to hold yourself to something that does not exist.

In his podcast on "Winning on the inside", John Maxwell says perfectionism paralyzes us. It keeps us from being creative, and it prevents us from getting started. Perfectionists are always waiting for the perfect answer or idea, which of course, does not exist. Often times perfectionists are perfectionists because they are worried about other people picking apart what they are doing. Perfectionism keeps us from being productive and distracts us from our purpose; it is not attainable and will only leave you disappointed.

For Nicki, being her best self means she embraces her emotions, good or bad, and has the tenacity to be able to reinvent herself in renewal. She allows her mind to be clear so intuition can flow to her. Nicki shares my sentiment that you do not have to be a public figure, CEO, or celebrity to live an extraordinary life. Nor do you have to break any glass ceilings. Rotary, which pays nothing, is a place where Nicki uses all of her gifts and feels most fulfilled. It is where her passion lies and what contributes to her being her best self.

Her words of advice are simple: Find your place for inspiration, whether it is in what you do or where you are most comfortable being open and honest with yourself. Create the space you need to determine your path. Moreover, when doing so, remember there is no need to be in a hurry. Enjoy the path.

She refers to a TED Talk by Daniele Quercia entitled "Happy Maps"[18]. In this talk, Daniele shares his discovery that all map apps lead us to our destination by giving us the shortest route possible, but we could be missing so much beauty and happiness by focusing so much effort on getting to our destination using the quickest route. He worked with some colleagues and together they built an app in England that not only connected people with the shortest route to their destination, but also gave options of the most beautiful, the happiest, and the quietest routes. Participants who used the app found the happy, the beautiful, and the quiet routes much more enjoyable than the quickest. Not only that, they related memories, smells, and experiences on these alternate routes. So when thinking about the path for your life, do not get so wrapped up in the destination that you forget about the journey, allow yourself to be less than perfect and remember that you are always enough.

What have we heard?

If you are anything like me, by the time you get to the end of the book, you will have forgotten so many of the things we have talked about. I was trying to come up with the best way to summarize our time together and of course, it came to me in poem. So before I leave you with your final application challenge, I would like to share this poem which touches on some of the important concepts we have discussed during our time together. It is called, you guessed it – Your Extraordinary Self

Your Extraordinary Self

How we choose to view the world will guide us through our life
Whether living days of glory or ones of passing strife,
The words we whisper in our head or choose to say aloud
Will lead us down a rainbow path or shadow us with clouds.
As we come upon the crossroads life no doubt will bring,
Choose the path that leads you to things that make your heart sing.
When it feels like your world is as fragile as cracked glass,
Step back, reflect, and breathe, for this too will surely pass.
We all get stuck at times, not knowing where next to go.
See it for the opportunity it is to revisit those values and goals.
Appreciate every moment by being present and aware.
Make a difference in people's lives by showing that you care.
Encourage and help others succeed in their ambitions too,
For abundance and prosperity is meant for more than simply you.
Surround yourself with lifters, and let toxic people go.
Face your fears and inhibitions head on, toe to toe.
Remember the illusion of perfection is simply a myth.
Celebrate your awesomeness and all the glory it brings with.
Forgive yourself and others for transgressions present and past.
Release those feelings of frustration and be carefree at long last.
When things go wrong or get off track, as they sometimes tend to do,
Look unto others and turn the focus back to you,
For you and only you control the choices that you make.
Your attitude about these choices will surely determine your fate.
In the end it's all about the one person you answer to,
And all the things that lead you to be your very best version of you.

Final Challenge

As we near the end of our journey together, I challenge you to reflect on the strategies and advice that have been shared throughout the book and really think about what living an extraordinary life means to you. As we have learned, when we are living a life of success, we are consistently showing up as our best selves—content, present, and aware—despite times of heartache or despair. Take a moment now to jot down the parts of the book that really resonated with you whether pieces of advice, the analogies that have been shared, or a revelation that came to you through the practical application or in reflection.

Once you are satisfied with your answer, copy it out on a separate piece of paper, something you can carry with you at all times, folded up, perhaps, in a purse or wallet or tucked under your pillow. Refer to it often, read it aloud, incorporate these things that resonate with you in all that you do. To be your extraordinary self, do more of what you love in life and whether you are having a great day or a horrible one, own it, live it, love it and always remember #anythingspossible!

About the Author

Tammie is an accomplished Executive and Board Member with more than twenty-three years of success across the insurance and leadership training industries. Leveraging extensive experience with start-ups, entrepreneurship, corporate growth, and training, she has helped many individuals with personal growth and companies with strategic planning, business process improvement, employee engagement and culture building. With a master's in public sector leadership from the Schulich School of Business, certificates in results leadership, strategic leadership, and executive leadership, a certified John Maxwell Leadership speaker, trainer and coach and author of *Your Extraordinary Self* Tammie is devoted to helping individuals and organizations achieve results by cultivating community, influencing change, championing leaders and increasing awareness within one's self and of others.

Throughout her career, she has been nominated for several leadership awards and has been awarded the CIP Society Emerging Leader Award, the Heather Grand Volunteer of the Year Award and named one of the Top 35 Women in Insurance by Insurance Business Canada Magazine. She regularly speaks both domestically and internationally on topics of leadership.

Tammie is the President of the Board of Directors for the Jennifer Ashleigh Children's Charity and Past President of the Ontario Insurance Adjusters Association. She is committed to giving back to the community through philanthropic efforts and will direct a portion of proceeds from the sale of this book to local charities and not-for-profits.

As a mother of two, a sister, daughter, and friend, Tammie has experienced exhilarating times, tumultuous times and everything in between. As a life-long learner herself, Tammie hopes that by writing this book and sharing these stories, readers will learn some new principles, validate some of the thoughts that they currently have and walk away with some strategies to make their lives extraordinary and if nothing else, to help them get through the difficult times in life. Tammie hopes the readers will relate to the stories shared because this is not a book about tips from multi-millionaires or famous people. It is a book about real everyday people just like them that manage to live extraordinary lives. She encourages readers to buy copies for their friends and family and to sell the book as a fundraiser for their child's sporting team or school drive for double the impact—raising money and adding value to others. Tammie wants readers to laugh a little, cry a little and nod their heads in agreement when they've read something profound. By writing this book, she is hoping to leave an imprint on the lives of others.

Bibliography

Allen, James. *As a Man Thinketh*. Mount Vernon, NY: Peter Pauper Press, 1951.

Covey, Stephen R. *7 Habits of Highly Effective People*. New York: Simon & Schuster, 1989.

Eker, T. Harv. *Secrets of the Millionaire Mind: Mastering the Inner Game of Wealth*. New York: HarperCollins, 2005.

Elliott, Louise. *The Brain Power Pyramid: 7 proven steps for how to Sleep like a Baby, Run like a Cheetah, Fuel like a Formula One Car, Create like Edison, Think like Da Vinci, Learn like Einstein And Network like a Rockstar!* Powell, OH: Author Academy Elite, 2018

Fenton, John. *5 Minute Mastery*. Grant Park Press, 2018.

Halvorson, Heidi Grant. *No One Understand You and What to Do About It*. Boston: HBR Press, 2015

Hill, Napoleon. *Think and Grow Rich*. New York: Fawcett Books, 1987.

Martin, William Fergus. *Four Steps to Forgiveness*. Rochester, Vermont: Findhorn Press, 2014

Maxwell, John. *Intentional Living: Choosing a Life that Matters.* New York: Hachette, 2015

———. *Failing Forward: Turning Mistakes into Stepping-Stones for Success.* Nashville: Thomas Nelson, 2007.

———. *21 Irrefutable Laws of Leadership: Follow Them and People Will Follow You.* Nashville: Thomas Nelson, 1998

Pasricha, Neil. *The Book of Awesome.* New York: Putnam, 2010.

———. *The Happiness Equation: Want Nothing + Do Anything = Have Everything.* New York: Putnam, 2016.

Peale, Norman Vincent. *The Power of Positive Thinking.* New York: Prentice-Hall, 1952

Sandberg, Sheryl. *Lean In: Women Work, and the Will to Lead.* New York: Alfred A, Knopf, 2013

Williamson, Marianne. *A Return to Love: Reflections on the Principles of A Course in Miracles.* New York: HarperCollins, 1992.

Notes

[1] Ken Robinson, "Do schools kill creativity?" TED: Ideas worth spreading. February 2006. https://www.ted.com/talks/ken_robinson_says_schools_kill_creativity?
[2] Dr. Lani Zlupko, "Staying Stuck or Moving Forward" TEDXWilmington. September 8, 2014. https://www.youtube.com/watch?v=sHLpOUZe388
[3] JC Norcross and DL Vangarelli, "The resolution solution: longitudinal examination of New Year's change attempts." University of Scranton. 1989. https://www.ncbi.nlm.nih.gov/pubmed/2980864
[4] Peter Economy, "7 Toxic People You Need to Get out of Your Life right Now." Inc. November 26, 2016.
[5] Napoleon Hill, Think and Grow Rich (New York: Fawcett Books, 1987), page.11–12
[6] "Wandering mind not a happy mind" The Harvard Gazette. November 11, 2010. https://news.harvard.edu/gazette/story/2010/11/wandering-mind-not-a-happy-mind/
[7] Travis Bradberry, "Emotional Intelligence – EQ" Forbes. January 9, 2014. https://www.forbes.com/sites/travisbradberry/2014/01/09/emotional-intelligence/#5402d4971ac0
[8] Sheryl Sandburg. Lean In: Women Work and the Will to Lead (New York: Alfred A. Knopf, 2013), page 26.

9. Laura Garnett, "4 Ways to Overcome Fear so You Can Achieve Your Dream." Inc. February 25, 2016. https://www.inc.com/laura-garnett/4-ways-to-overcome-fear-so-you-can-achieve-your-dreams.html
10. Jessica Stillman, "Gratitude Physically Changes Your Brain" Inc. January 15, 2016. https://www.inc.com/jessica-stillman/the-amazing-way-gratitude-rewires-your-brain-for-happiness.html
11. John Maxwell, Intentional Living: Choosing a Life that Matters (New York: Hachette, 2015), page 15.
12. Stephen Covey, 7 Habits of Highly Effective People (New York: Simon & Schuster, 1989), page.230–231
13. "7 Scientific Facts About the Benefit of Doing Good" Goodnet: Gateway To Doing Good. January 26, 2017 https://www.goodnet.org/articles/7-scientific-facts-about-benefit-doing-good
14. Jerf W.K. Yeung, Zhuoni Zhang, and Tae Yeun Kim, "Volunteering and health benefits in general adults: cumulative effects and forms" BCM Public Health. July 11, 2017. https://bmcpublichealth.biomedcentral.com/articles/10.1186/s12889-017-4561-8
15. John Maxwell, Failing Forward: Turning Mistakes into Stepping-Stones for Success (Nashville: Thomas Nelson, 2007), 27–30
16. William Fergus Martin. Four Steps to Forgiveness (Rochester, Vermont: Findhorn Press, 2014), page 8.
17. Marianne Williamson, A Return to Love: Reflections on the Principles of A Course in Miracles (New York: HarperCollins, 1992), 190–191
18. Daniele Quercia, "Happy Maps?" TED: Ideas worth spreading. January 6, 2015. https://www.ted.com/talks/daniele_quercia_happy_maps?language=en

Manufactured by Amazon.ca
Bolton, ON